taste of home
Desserts

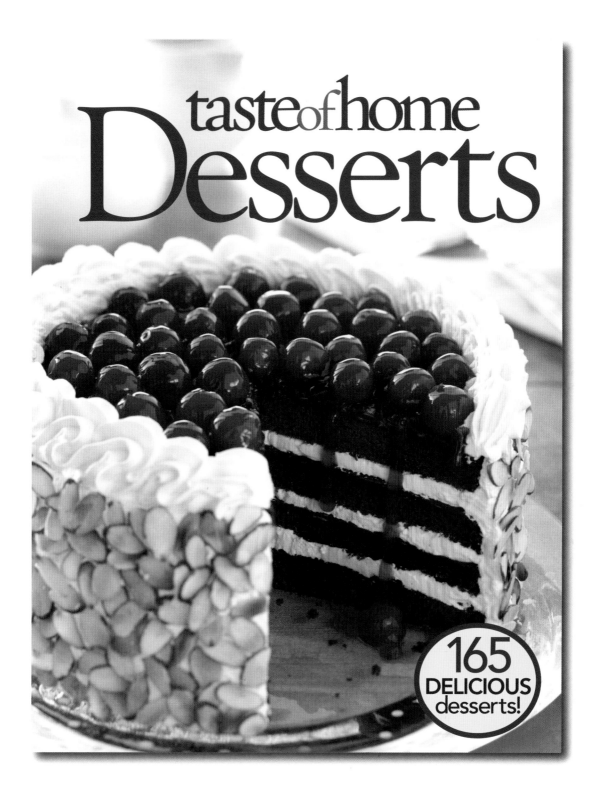

165 DELICIOUS desserts!

taste of home
Desserts

Senior Vice President, Editor in Chief: Catherine Cassidy
Vice President, Executive Editor/Books: Heidi Reuter Lloyd
Creative Director: Ardyth Cope
Food Director: Diane Werner RD
Senior Editor/Books: Mark Hagen
Editor: Amy Glander
Art Directors: Rudy Krochalk, Gretchen Trautman
Content Production Supervisor: Julie Wagner
Layout Designers: Kathy Crawford, Nancy Novak
Proofreader: Linne Bruskewitz
Recipe Asset Management System: Coleen Martin, Sue A. Jurack
Premedia Supervisor: Scott Berger
Recipe Testing and Editing: Taste of Home Test Kitchen
Food Photography: Reiman Photo Studio
Editorial Assistant: Barb Czysz
Cover Photo Photographer: Rob Hagen
Cover Photo Set Stylist: Grace Natoli-Sheldon
Cover Photo Food Stylist: Jim Rude

Chief Marketing Officer: Lisa Karpinski
Vice President/Book Marketing: Dan Fink
Creative Director/Creative Marketing: Jim Palmen

The Reader's Digest Association, Inc.

President and Chief Executive Officer: Mary G. Berner
President, Food & Entertaining: Suzanne M. Grimes
President, Consumer Marketing: Dawn Zier

Pictured on front cover: Black Forest Torte (p. 37)
Pictured on back cover: Coconut Chiffon Pie (p. 18), Raspberry-Fudge Frozen Dessert (p. 101), Chocolate Cupcakes (p. 82), Chocolate Cinamon Mud Balls (p. 48)

International Standard Book Number (10): 0-89821-747-4
International Standard Book Number (13): 978-0-89821-747-6
Library of Congress Control Number: 2009924398

Great Gift!

Taste of Home Desserts makes a great gift for those who are passionate for sweets or simply love baking. To order additional copies, specify item number 39115 and send $14.99 (plus $4.99 shipping/processing for one book, $5.99 for two or more) to: Shop Taste of Home, Suite 1106, P.O. Box 26820, Lehigh Valley, PA 18002-6280. To order by credit card, call toll-free 1-800/880-3012.

Table of Contents

black forest cheesecake, p. 60

it's a sweet, sweet life...

freezer peanut butter pie, p. 99

Taste of Home Desserts

Your One-Stop-Shop For All Things Divine!

*Life is too short to pass up dessert. So why not surrender to temptation with a heavenly slice of a rich, velvety cheesecake or a spoonful of a frosty delight? We all have that one guilty pleasure we simply cannot resist, and with the sumptuous assortment of 165 sweet sensations in **Taste of Home Desserts**, you're sure to find that oh-so-perfect showstopper for any occasion.*

If you're passionate for all things smooth and creamy, take a big bite into Raspberry Ribbon Cheesecake (p. 14) or a host of other dreamy recipes featuring cheesecake in all its lusciousness. If it's pure chocolate you crave, you can't go wrong with Chocolate Cream Bonbons (p. 40) or Chocolate Lover's Chiffon Cake (p. 44). Is your taste on the sophisticated side? Turn your kitchen into a patisserie with elegant desserts such as Dobostorte (p. 61) or Genoise with Fruit & Cream Filling (p. 25). And nothing says "home sweet home" like the aroma of a freshly baked pie or a tender cake fresh from the oven. Delight in tried-and-true home-style classics like Star-Studded Blueberry Pie (p. 20) or Black Forest Torte (p. 37).

In addition to these divine pleasures, you'll also find flaky, cream-filled pastries, bite-sized candies and confections, icy indulgences, sky-high trifles and tortes, blissful brownies and bars, and other tantalizing, melt-in-your-mouth wonders that taste as irresistible as they sound.

Rich, full-color photos offer visual inspiration, and handy dessert-making tips make even the most over-the-top recipe doable. From old-fashioned favorites to lip-smacking novelties, **Desserts** is guaranteed to earn you cheers and keep your sweet tooth forever satisfied!

a little slice of heaven

Take just one bite into any of the divine desserts in this chapter, and you'll find yourself in the promised land of all things sweet. Whether it's a cool, refreshing pie, a tangy, fruit-filled tart or a lush, silky cheesecake topped with fluffy whipped cream, you simply won't be able to resist the to-die-for baked goodness on the pages that follow.

hazelnut pear tart

hazelnut pear tart

Anne Addesso • Sheboygan, Wisconsin
This pretty, pleasing pear tart seems like it came from a fancy bakery. Destined to become a favorite holiday dessert, it looks and smells as delightful as it tastes.

1	cup butter, softened
1/2	cup confectioners' sugar
1	teaspoon vanilla extract
2	cups all-purpose flour
1/2	cup chopped blanched hazelnuts

FILLING:

1/3	cup apricot preserves
2/3	cup chopped blanched hazelnuts, toasted
1/2	cup sugar
1	tablespoon all-purpose flour
6	tablespoons butter, softened
1	egg, lightly beaten
2-3/4	pounds pears, peeled and sliced

In a large bowl, cream butter and confectioners' sugar until light and fluffy. Beat in the vanilla. Gradually add flour; stir in hazelnuts.

Press into a greased 11-in. fluted tart pan with removable bottom. Bake at 400° for 10 minutes. Remove from the oven; reduce heat to 350°.

Spread apricot preserves over crust. In a large bowl, combine the hazelnuts, sugar, flour, butter and egg. Spoon over preserves. Arrange pear slices over filling in a concentric circle, slightly overlapping slices.

Bake tart for 40-45 minutes or until golden brown. Cool on a wire rack. Store in the refrigerator. **yield: 10-12 servings.**

chocolate-marbled cheesecake dessert

Marjorie Runyan • Middleburg, Pennsylvania
This luscious cheesecake features three kinds of chocolate—baking cocoa, hot fudge topping and chocolate chips. A small piece is all you need to round out a festive dinner.

1/2	cup butter, softened
1	cup sugar, *divided*
1	cup all-purpose flour
1/4	cup baking cocoa
1/4	teaspoon salt
2	packages (8 ounces *each*) cream cheese, softened
2	eggs, lightly beaten
1	teaspoon vanilla extract
1/2	cup hot fudge ice cream topping
1/4	cup semisweet chocolate chips, melted

Milk chocolate *or* striped chocolate kisses, optional

In a small bowl, cream butter and 1/2 cup sugar until light and fluffy. Combine the flour, cocoa and salt; gradually add to creamed mixture and mix well. Press into a greased 8-in. square baking dish; set aside.

In a large bowl, beat cream cheese and remaining sugar until smooth. Add eggs and vanilla; beat on low speed just until combined. Remove 1 cup to a small bowl; beat in fudge topping. Spread 1 cup over crust; spread with remaining cream cheese mixture.

Stir melted chips into remaining fudge mixture; drop by teaspoonfuls over cream cheese layer. Cut through batter with a knife to swirl.

Bake at 350° for 40-45 minutes or until a toothpick inserted near the center comes out clean. Cool on a wire rack. Garnish with kisses if desired. Store in the refrigerator. **yield: 12-16 servings.**

chocolate-marbled cheesecake dessert

lemon mascarpone cheesecake

DESSERT *Tip*

To judge the doneness of cheesecake, tap the side of the pan with a wooden spoon to measure the center of the cheesecake's "jiggle." Generally, it should be about the size of a walnut. Remember that cheesecakes do not set up completely until they are thoroughly cooled or chilled.

Lorraine Caland
Thunder Bay, Ontario
The light color and mild lemon flavor of this cheesecake makes it a lovely treat for spring.

lemon mascarpone cheesecake

1-1/2 **cups biscotti crumbs (about 8 biscotti)**
1/3 **cup butter, melted**
FILLING:
2 **packages (8 ounces *each*) cream cheese, softened**
2 **cartons (8 ounces *each*) Mascarpone cheese**
3/4 **cup sugar**
1/4 **cup lemon juice**
3 **tablespoons all-purpose flour**
2 **teaspoons vanilla extract**
4 **eggs, lightly beaten**
1 **tablespoon grated lemon peel**
TOPPING:
3/4 **cup coarsely chopped dried apricots**
1/2 **cup boiling water**
3/4 **cup cold water**
1/4 **cup sugar**
1/4 **cup orange marmalade**
2 **squares (1 ounce *each*) white baking chocolate**

In a small bowl, combine biscotti crumbs and butter. Press onto the bottom and 1 in. up the sides of a greased 9-in. springform pan.

Place on a baking sheet. Bake crust at 350° for 8-10 minutes or until lightly browned.

In a large bowl, beat the cheeses, sugar, lemon juice, flour and vanilla until smooth. Add eggs; beat on low speed just until combined. Stir in lemon peel. Pour into crust.

Return pan to baking sheet. Bake at 350° for 45-55 minutes or until center is almost set. Cool on a wire rack for 10 minutes. Carefully run a knife around edge of pan to loosen. Cool for 30 minutes.

Meanwhile, soak apricots in boiling water for 10 minutes. Drain and discard liquid. In a small saucepan, bring the apricots, cold water and sugar to a boil. Reduce heat; simmer, uncovered, for 12-14 minutes or until water is absorbed. Remove from the heat; stir in marmalade. Cool to room temperature.

Carefully spread topping over cheesecake; cool 30 minutes longer. Refrigerate overnight.

Remove sides of pan. In a microwave-safe bowl, melt white chocolate at 70% power for 1 minute; stir. Microwave at additional 10- to 20-second intervals, stirring until smooth. Drizzle over cheesecake. Let stand for 15 minutes. Refrigerate leftovers. **yield: 14 servings.**

blackberry cheese pie

cherry banana cream pie

Denise Elder • Hanover, Ontario
This dessert has a crunchy crust spread with a rich butter layer, topped with a filling flavored with banana, cherries and chocolate. Guests tell me the pie reminds them of a banana split...and then ask for seconds.

>   3/4 cup butter, *divided*
>   2 cups crushed vanilla wafers (about 60 wafers)
>   3/4 cup confectioners' sugar
> FILLING:
>   1 cup heavy whipping cream
>   1/4 cup sugar
>   2 tablespoons baking cocoa
>   1 cup chopped walnuts
>   1 large firm banana, thinly sliced
>   1/3 cup halved maraschino cherries
> Whipped topping, chocolate curls and additional
>   maraschino cherries

In a small saucepan, melt 1/2 cup of butter; stir in wafer crumbs. Press into a 9-in. pie plate. In a small bowl, cream the remaining butter and confectioners' sugar until light and fluffy. Spread over crust.

In a large bowl, beat cream until it begins to thicken. Add the sugar and cocoa; beat until stiff peaks form. Fold in the walnuts, banana and maraschino cherries.

Spoon into crust. Cover and refrigerate for 8 hours or overnight. Garnish with whipped topping, chocolate curls and cherries. **yield: 6-8 servings.**

blackberry cheese pie

Taste of Home Test Kitchen • Greendale, Wisconsin
This pie is great to serve at church potlucks because it has a memorable look and taste. The citrus tang really goes well with the colorful berries and velvety cream cheese filling.

> Pastry for single-crust pie (9 inches)
>   2 packages (3 ounces *each*) cream cheese,
>   softened
>   1/3 cup confectioners' sugar
>   1/3 cup heavy whipping cream, whipped
>   3/4 cup sugar
>   1/4 cup cornstarch
>   1 cup pineapple-orange juice
>   2 cups fresh blackberries *and/or* raspberries,
>   *divided*

Line a 9-in. pie plate with pastry; trim and flute edges. Line pastry shell with a double thickness of heavy-duty foil. Bake at 450° for 8 minutes. Remove foil; bake 5 minutes longer. Cool on a wire rack.

In a small bowl, beat cream cheese and confectioners' sugar. Fold in whipped cream. Transfer to pastry shell. Refrigerate for 30 minutes.

In a small saucepan, combine sugar and cornstarch. Gradually whisk in juice until smooth. Bring to a boil; cook and stir for 2 minutes or until thickened. Remove from the heat.

Mash 1/2 cup berries; stir into juice mixture. Cool for 10 minutes, stirring several times. Fold in remaining berries. Spoon over cream cheese mixture.

Cover and refrigerate for at least 4 hours. Refrigerate leftovers. **yield: 6-8 servings.**

yogurt berry pies

Dawn Fagerstrom • Warren, Minnesota
These pies are a snap to assemble because they call for only two ingredients in the filling, yet they look and taste like you fussed. Topped with fresh blueberries and raspberries, they're simply irresistible.

>   1 carton (8 ounces) mixed berry yogurt *or*
>   flavor of your choice
>   2 cups whipped topping
>   1 package (6 count) individual graham cracker
>   tart shells
> Blueberries and raspberries

In a large bowl, stir the yogurt and whipped topping until combined. Spoon into tart shells. Cover and freeze for 20 minutes or until set. Top with berries. **yield: 6 servings.**

pear crunch pie

mocha almond dessert

Taste of Home Test Kitchen • Greendale, Wisconsin
For an easy, make-ahead dessert that's elegant and luscious, try this recipe from our home economists. The perfect blend of mocha and chocolate is in each cool, refreshing slice.

- 1 cup cream-filled chocolate sandwich cookie crumbs
- 1/4 cup sugar
- 1/4 cup butter, melted
- 1 package (8 ounces) cream cheese, softened
- 1 can (14 ounces) sweetened condensed milk
- 2/3 cup chocolate syrup
- 1/2 teaspoon vanilla extract
- 2 tablespoons instant coffee granules
- 1 tablespoon hot water
- 1 cup whipped topping
- 1/3 cup chopped almonds, toasted

Chocolate-covered coffee beans, optional

In a small bowl, combine the cookie crumbs, sugar and butter. Press onto the bottom and 1 in. up the sides of a greased 9-in. springform pan; set aside.

In a large bowl, beat the cream cheese, milk, chocolate syrup and vanilla until smooth. Dissolve coffee granules in hot water; beat into cream cheese mixture. Fold in whipped topping and almonds. Pour over crust. Cover and freeze for 8 hours or overnight.

Remove from the freezer 10-15 minutes before serving. Carefully run a knife around edge of pan to loosen. Garnish with chocolate-covered coffee beans if desired. **yield: 10-12 servings.**

pear crunch pie

Marian Platt • Sequim, Washington
This recipe is one of my favorites. The pecan topping gives a nice crunch to this heavenly pie.

- 1 cup all-purpose flour
- 1/2 cup packed brown sugar
- 1/2 teaspoon ground nutmeg, *divided*
- 1/4 teaspoon ground cinnamon
- 1/2 cup plus 1 tablespoon cold butter, *divided*
- 1/2 cup chopped pecans
- 2 cans (15-1/4 ounces *each*) pear halves in syrup
- 1/4 cup sugar
- 2 tablespoons cornstarch
- 1/4 teaspoon salt
- 1 tablespoon lemon juice
- 1 teaspoon grated lemon peel
- 1 unbaked pastry shell (9 inches)

In a large bowl, combine the flour, brown sugar, 1/4 teaspoon of the nutmeg and cinnamon. Cut in 1/2 cup butter until mixture resembles coarse crumbs; stir in nuts. Set aside.

Drain pears, reserving 1 cup juice. In a large saucepan, combine the sugar, cornstarch, salt, remaining nutmeg and reserved juice until smooth. Bring to a boil; cook and stir for 2 minutes or until thickened. Remove from the heat; stir in the lemon juice, lemon peel and remaining butter.

Cut pears in half; arrange in pastry shell. Pour sauce over pears; sprinkle with reserved nut topping. Bake at 375° for 50-55 minutes or until golden brown. **yield: 6-8 servings.**

mocha almond dessert

classic lemon meringue pie

Lee Bremson • Kansas City, Missouri

This is the one and only lemon meringue pie recipe you'll ever need. The flaky and tender from-scratch crust is worth the effort.

1-1/3	cups all-purpose flour
1/2	teaspoon salt
1/2	cup shortening
3	tablespoons plus 1/2 cup cold water, *divided*
2	tablespoons sugar
1	tablespoon cornstarch

FILLING:

1-1/4	cups sugar
1/4	cup cornstarch
3	tablespoons all-purpose flour
1/4	teaspoon salt
1-1/2	cups water
3	egg yolks, lightly beaten
2	tablespoons butter
1-1/2	teaspoons grated lemon peel
1/3	cup lemon juice

MERINGUE:

4	egg whites
3/4	teaspoon vanilla extract
6	tablespoons sugar

In a small bowl, combine flour and salt; cut in shortening until crumbly. Gradually add 3 tablespoons cold water, tossing with a fork until dough forms a ball.

classic lemon meringue pie

Roll out pastry to fit a 9-in. pie plate. Transfer pastry to pie plate. Trim to 1/2 in. beyond edge of plate; flute edges. Bake crust at 425° for 12-15 minutes or until lightly browned.

In a small saucepan, combine sugar and cornstarch. Gradually stir in remaining cold water until smooth. Bring to a boil over medium heat; cook and stir for 1 minute or until mixture is thickened and clear. Remove from the heat; set aside to cool.

For filling, in a large saucepan, combine the sugar, cornstarch, flour and salt. Gradually stir in water until smooth. Cook and stir over medium-high heat until thickened and bubbly. Reduce heat; cook and stir 2 minutes longer.

Remove from the heat. Stir a small amount of hot filling into egg yolks; return all to the pan, stirring constantly. Bring to a gentle boil; cook and stir 2 minutes longer. Remove from the heat. Gently stir in butter and lemon peel. Gradually stir in lemon juice just until combined. Pour into the crust.

In a large bowl, beat egg whites and vanilla on medium speed until soft peaks form. Gradually beat in sugar, 1 tablespoon at a time, on high. Beat in reserved cornstarch mixture on high until stiff, glossy peaks form and sugar is dissolved. Spread evenly over hot filling, sealing edges to crust.

Bake at 350° for 25 minutes or until meringue is golden brown. Cool on a wire rack for 1 hour. Refrigerate for at least 3 hours before serving. Refrigerate leftovers. **yield: 6-8 servings.**

toffee apple pie

Dixie Helders • Roberts, Wisconsin

Fruit trees in my yard provide me with the main ingredient for this lovely pie. A scoop of vanilla or cinnamon ice cream is terrific on top.

5	cups sliced peeled Granny Smith apples
1/2	cup sugar
1/2	cup packed brown sugar
1	Heath candy bar (1.4 ounces), chopped
2	tablespoons cornstarch
1	tablespoon butter, melted
1	teaspoon ground cinnamon

Dash ground nutmeg

1	unbaked pastry shell (9 inches)

TOPPING:

1/3	cup all-purpose flour
2	tablespoons brown sugar

1/4   teaspoon ground cinnamon
   2   tablespoons cold butter
1/4   cup chopped nuts
   1   Heath candy bar (1.4 ounces), chopped

In a large bowl, combine the first eight ingredients. Spoon into pie shell. For topping, combine the flour, brown sugar and cinnamon; cut in butter until the mixture resembles coarse crumbs. Add nuts and chopped candy bar. Sprinkle over pie.

Bake at 375° for 30-35 minutes or until topping is browned and apples are tender. **yield: 6-8 servings.**

strawberry cheesecake pie

Janis Plourde • Smooth Rock Falls, Ontario
This creamy concoction is so refreshing on a hot day and also really easy to assemble. Company will never know how simple this luscious pie is to prepare.

   2   cups sliced fresh strawberries
1/4   cup chopped almonds, toasted
   1   tablespoon sugar
   1   graham cracker crust (9 inches)
   1   package (8 ounces) cream cheese, softened
   2   cups cold milk, *divided*
   1   package (3.4 ounces) instant vanilla
        pudding mix

In a small bowl, combine the strawberries, almonds and sugar. Pour into crust; set aside. In a large bowl, beat cream cheese until smooth; gradually add 1/2 cup of

strawberry cheesecake pie

apple cranberry tart

milk. Add pudding mix and remaining milk. Beat for 1 minute or until blended; pour over strawberries. Cover and refrigerate for 2 hours or until set. **yield: 8 servings.**

apple cranberry tart

Suzanne Strocsher • Bothell, Washington
You'll love the tangy sweetness of this quick but elegant-looking dessert. Serve alongside vanilla ice cream and watch this easy-to-make treat as it's gobbled up in no time!

Pastry for double-crust pie (9 inches)
   2   cups fresh *or* frozen cranberries, coarsely
        chopped
   2   medium tart apples, peeled and coarsely
        chopped
1-1/4   cups packed brown sugar
   2   tablespoons all-purpose flour
1/2   teaspoon ground cinnamon
   1   to 2 tablespoons butter

On a lightly floured surface, roll half of the pastry into a 13-in. circle. Press onto the bottom and up the sides of an ungreased 11-in. fluted tart pan with removable bottom or press onto the bottom and 1 in. up the sides of a 10-in. springform pan.

In a large bowl, combine the cranberries, apples, brown sugar, flour and cinnamon; pour into crust. Dot with butter. Cut leaf shapes from the remaining pastry. Place over filling.

Place the tart pan on a baking sheet. Bake at 425° for 35-40 minutes or until filling is hot and bubbly and the crust is golden. Cool on a wire rack. Serve warm. **yield: 12-16 servings.**

Peggy Frazier
Indianapolis, Indiana
Here's a mouth-watering dessert that's sure to impress family and friends. Not only does it taste wonderful with its chocolate cookie crust, rich, creamy cheesecake and tangy raspberry center and topping...it also looks lovely!

raspberry ribbon cheesecake

2	**cups chocolate wafer crumbs**
1/3	**cup butter, melted**
3	**tablespoons sugar**

RASPBERRY SAUCE:

2-1/2	**cups fresh *or* frozen unsweetened raspberries, thawed**
2/3	**cup sugar**
2	**tablespoons cornstarch**
2	**teaspoons lemon juice**

FILLING/TOPPING:

3	**packages (8 ounces *each*) cream cheese, softened**
1/2	**cup sugar**
2	**tablespoons all-purpose flour**
1	**teaspoon vanilla extract**
2	**egg whites**
1	**cup heavy whipping cream**
2	**to 3 tablespoons orange juice**
1-1/2	**cups fresh *or* frozen unsweetened raspberries, thawed**

Combine the first three ingredients; press into bottom and 1-1/2 in. up sides of a greased 9-in. springform pan. Chill 1 hour or until firm.

In a blender, cover and process raspberries until pureed. Press through a sieve; discard seeds. Add water if necessary to measure 1 cup.

In a small saucepan, combine sugar and cornstarch. Stir in raspberry juice; bring to a boil. Cook and stir for 2 minutes or until thickened. Remove from heat; stir in lemon juice and set aside.

In a large bowl, beat the cream cheese, sugar, flour and vanilla until smooth. Add egg whites; beat on low just until blended. Stir in cream.

Pour half into crust. Top with 3/4 cup raspberry sauce (cover and refrigerate remaining sauce). Carefully spoon remaining filling over the sauce.

Bake at 375° for 35-40 minutes or until center is nearly set. Remove from oven; immediately run a knife around pan to loosen crust. Cool on wire rack 1 hour.

Refrigerate overnight. Add orange juice to chilled raspberry sauce; gently fold in the raspberries. Spoon over the cheesecake. **yield: 12-16 servings.**

autumn apple tart

Grace Howaniec • Waukesha, Wisconsin
There are so many apple orchards in our state, and this tasty tart is one of my favorite ways to use this abundant fall fruit.

CRUST:
- 1-1/4 cups all-purpose flour
- 1 tablespoon sugar
- 1 teaspoon baking powder
- 1/2 teaspoon salt
- 1/2 cup butter, cubed
- 1 egg, lightly beaten
- 2 tablespoons milk
- 6 medium tart apples, peeled and cut into 1/4-inch slices

TOPPING:
- 1/3 to 1/2 cup sugar
- 2 tablespoons butter
- 1/2 teaspoon ground cinnamon
- 1/2 teaspoon ground nutmeg
- 1-1/2 tablespoons all-purpose flour

In a large bowl, combine the flour, sugar, baking powder and salt. Cut in butter until mixture resembles fine crumbs. Combine egg and milk; stir into flour mixture until blended.

Press onto the bottom and up the sides of an ungreased 11-in. tart pan with removable bottom. Arrange apple slices over crust.

In a small bowl, combine topping ingredients; sprinkle over apples. Place pan on a baking sheet. Bake at 350° for 50-60 minutes or until apples are tender. Serve warm or cool. **yield: 12 servings.**

autumn apple tart

lemon tart

lemon tart

Erlene Cornelius • Spring City, Tennessee
Smooth and creamy, with a refreshing lemon taste, this tart gets rave reviews. Every time I serve it to someone new, it results in a request for the recipe.

- 1 cup sugar
- 1/4 cup cornstarch
- 1 cup milk
- 3 egg yolks, lightly beaten
- 1/4 cup butter
- 1 tablespoon grated lemon peel
- 1/3 cup lemon juice
- 1 cup (8 ounces) sour cream
- 1 pastry shell (9 inches), baked
- Whipped topping

In a large saucepan, combine sugar and cornstarch. Gradually add milk until smooth. Cook and stir over medium-high heat until thickened. Reduce heat; cook and stir 2 minutes longer. Remove from the heat. Stir a small amount of hot liquid into egg yolks; return all to the pan. Bring to a gentle boil, stirring constantly. Cook 2 minutes longer (mixture will be very thick).

Remove from the heat; stir in butter and lemon peel. Gently stir in the lemon juice. Cover and cool completely.

Fold in sour cream. Pour into pastry shell. Refrigerate for at least 2 hours before cutting. Garnish with whipped topping. **yield: 6-8 servings.**

candy cane cheesecake

Gwen Koob-Roach • Saskatoon, Saskatchewan
This pepperminty cheesecake says "Christmas" at first sight and first bite. The recipe earned me a dairy producer's scholarship. Now, it regularly wins compliments at seasonal parties and teas.

```
1-1/2   cups chocolate wafer crumbs
  1/3   cup butter, melted
    2   tablespoons sugar
```
FILLING:
```
    3   packages (8 ounces each) cream cheese,
        softened
  3/4   cup sugar
    3   tablespoons all-purpose flour
    4   eggs
    1   cup (8 ounces) sour cream
    2   tablespoons vanilla or white chips
  1/2   to 3/4 teaspoon peppermint extract
```
Red liquid or paste food coloring
Crushed peppermint candy and whipped topping,
  optional

Combine the first three ingredients; press onto the bottom of a 9-in. springform pan. Chill. In a bowl, beat cream cheese and sugar until smooth; add flour and mix well. Add the eggs, one at a time, beating just until blended. Stir in sour cream. Set aside.

In a small saucepan over low heat, melt vanilla chips. Remove from the heat. Add 1/4 cup cream cheese mixture, extract and a few drops of food coloring; mix well. Pour half of the remaining cream cheese mixture over crust. Top with half of the peppermint mixture; swirl with a knife. Repeat layers.

candy cane cheesecake

Bake at 325° for 35-40 minutes longer or until the center is almost set. Cool on a wire rack for 10 minutes. Carefully run a knife around the edge of the pan; cool 1 hour longer.

Refrigerate overnight. Just before serving, remove sides of pan. Garnish cheesecake with crushed candy and whipped topping if desired. Refrigerate leftovers. **yield: 12-16 servings.**

cherry-lemon icebox pie

Mary Weller • Twin Lake, Michigan
This recipe makes a nice and refreshing finish to a hearty meal. The cherry and lemon flavors combine for a mouth-watering taste sensation.

Pastry for single-crust pie (9 inches)
```
    1   can (14 ounces) sweetened condensed milk
  1/2   cup lemon juice
  1/2   teaspoon vanilla extract
  1/2   teaspoon almond extract
1-1/2   cups heavy whipping cream
    1   can (21 ounces) cherry pie filling
```

Line a 9-in. deep-dish pie plate with pastry; trim and flute edges. Line pastry shell with a double thickness of heavy-duty foil. Bake at 450° for 8 minutes. Remove foil; bake 5-7 minutes longer or until lightly browned. Cool on a wire rack.

In a large bowl, whisk the milk, lemon juice and extracts until thickened, about 2 minutes. Beat cream until stiff peaks form; fold into milk mixture. Pour into crust.

Refrigerate for 30 minutes; spoon pie filling over the top. Refrigerate for at least 2 hours before serving. **yield: 8 servings.**

mini caramel cheesecakes

Taste of Home Test Kitchen • Greendale, Wisconsin
Using individual graham cracker shells makes it easy to prepare these treats. They taste just like real cheesecake without all the hassle.

```
    1   package (8 ounces) cream cheese, softened
    2   tablespoons apple juice concentrate
    2   tablespoons sugar
  1/4   cup caramel ice cream topping
  1/2   cup whipped topping
    1   package (6 count) individual graham cracker
        tart shells
```

mini caramel cheesecakes

Pour over the brownie crust. Top with melted chocolate; cut through batter with a knife to swirl the chocolate.

Bake at 350° for 35-40 minutes or until center is almost set. Run a knife around edge of pan to loosen; cool completely. Remove sides of pan; refrigerate for at least 3 hours. Garnish with whipped cream and chocolate kisses if desired. **yield: 8-10 servings.**

cran-raspberry pie

Verona Koehlmoos • Pilger, Nebraska
Jewel-toned fruits team up to pack this lattice-topped pie. It's a lovely addition to any meal, big or small.

- 2 cups chopped fresh *or* frozen cranberries
- 5 cups fresh *or* frozen unsweetened raspberries, thawed
- 1/2 teaspoon almond extract
- 1 to 1-1/4 cups sugar
- 1/4 cup quick-cooking tapioca
- 1/4 teaspoon salt

Pastry for double-crust pie (9 inches)

In a large bowl, combine the cranberries, raspberries and extract. Combine the sugar, tapioca and salt. Add to fruit mixture; toss gently to coat. Let stand for 15-20 minutes.

Line pie plate with bottom pastry; trim to 1 in. beyond edge of plate. Add filling. Roll out remaining pastry; make a lattice crust. Trim, seal and flute edges. Cover edges loosely with foil.

Bake at 375° for 40-45 minutes or until crust is golden brown and filling is bubbly. Cool on a wire rack. **yield: 6-8 servings.**

Additional caramel ice cream topping, optional
Chopped almonds *or* honey roasted almonds, optional

In a large bowl, beat the cream cheese, apple juice concentrate, sugar and ice cream topping until smooth. Fold in whipped topping.

Spoon filling into tart shells. Drizzle with additional ice cream topping and sprinkle with almonds if desired. Refrigerate until serving. **yield: 6 servings.**

brownie swirl cheesecake

Janet Brunner • Burlington, Kentucky
It may look fancy, but this cheesecake is so simple. The secret is the speedy crust made from a packaged brownie mix. You don't need to be an experienced baker to make the elegant chocolate swirls on top—anyone can do it!

- 1 package (8 ounces) brownie mix
- 2 packages (8 ounces *each*) cream cheese, softened
- 1/2 cup sugar
- 1 teaspoon vanilla extract
- 2 eggs
- 1 cup milk chocolate chips, melted

Whipped cream and miniature chocolate kisses, optional

Prepare brownie mix according to package directions for chewy fudge brownies. Spread into a greased 9-in. springform pan. Bake at 350° for 15 minutes (brownies will not test done). Cool for 10 minutes on a wire rack.

Meanwhile, in a bowl, combine the cream cheese, sugar and vanilla. Add eggs, one at a time, beating well after each addition.

cran-raspberry pie

coconut chiffon pie

coconut chiffon pie

Kristine Fry • Fennimore, Wisconsin

A slice of this smooth, silky pie is pure pleasure. I like to garnish it with wide curls of fresh coconut for a little extra dazzle.

- 1 unbaked pastry shell (9 inches)
- 1 envelope unflavored gelatin
- 1/4 cup cold water
- 1/2 cup sugar
- 1/4 cup all-purpose flour
- 1/2 teaspoon salt
- 1-1/2 cups milk
- 3/4 teaspoon vanilla extract
- 1/4 teaspoon almond extract
- 1 cup heavy whipping cream, whipped
- 1 cup flaked coconut

Shaved fresh coconut, optional

Line unpricked pastry shell with a double thickness of heavy-duty foil. Bake at 450° for 8 minutes. Remove foil; bake 5 minutes longer. Cool on a wire rack.

Sprinkle gelatin over cold water; let stand for 1 minute. In a small saucepan, combine the sugar, flour and salt. Gradually stir in milk until smooth. Cook and stir over medium-low heat until mixture comes to a boil; cook and stir 1 minute longer or until thickened.

Remove from the heat. Whisk in gelatin mixture until dissolved. Transfer to a large bowl. Refrigerate until slightly thickened, about 30 minutes.

Add extracts; beat on medium speed for 1 minute. Fold in whipped cream and flaked coconut. Spread into pie crust. Refrigerate for at least 3 hours before serving. Garnish pie with shaved fresh coconut if desired. **yield: 6-8 servings.**

spiced peach pie

Lois Dunlop • Venice, Florida

Chilled peach pie is a delectable change of pace from the traditional baked fruit pie. With its peachy gelatin filling sandwiched between layers of fluffy cream, this pie slices beautifully and always draws compliments.

- 1 can (15 ounces) sliced peaches
- 2 tablespoons brown sugar
- 1/4 teaspoon ground ginger
- 1 cinnamon stick (3 inches)
- 1 package (3 ounces) peach gelatin *or* orange gelatin
- 4 ounces cream cheese, softened
- 2 tablespoons butter, softened
- 1/8 teaspoon ground nutmeg
- 1 pastry shell (9 inches), baked
- 1 carton (8 ounces) frozen whipped topping, thawed

Fresh mint, optional

Drain syrup from peaches into a 2-cup measuring cup. Add enough water to measure 1-1/3 cups. Chop peaches and set aside.

In a large saucepan, combine the syrup, brown sugar, ginger and cinnamon stick. Bring to a boil. Reduce heat; cook and stir for 5 minutes. Remove from the heat.

Discard cinnamon stick. Stir gelatin into syrup mixture until dissolved. Add peaches. Refrigerate until partially set, about 40 minutes.

In a large bowl, beat the cream cheese, butter and nutmeg until smooth. Spread over the bottom and up

spiced peach pie

the sides of the crust. Pour gelatin mixture over cream cheese layer.

Chill until serving. Spread with whipped topping. Serve with mint if desired. **yield: 6-8 servings.**

rhubarb meringue pie

Theresa Connell • Puyallup, Washington
My husband and brother, former "rhubarb haters," now can't wait for the first stalks of the plant to appear, heralding spring and their favorite pie!

CRUST:
- 1/2 cup butter, softened
- 1/4 cup sugar
- 1 teaspoon vanilla extract
- 1 cup all-purpose flour
- 3/4 cup quick-cooking oats
- 1/2 teaspoon salt

FILLING:
- 3 cups diced fresh *or* frozen rhubarb
- 1 tablespoon water
- 1 cup sugar
- 2 tablespoons all-purpose flour
- 1/8 teaspoon salt
- 3 egg yolks, lightly beaten

MERINGUE:
- 3 egg whites
- 1/8 teaspoon salt
- 1/3 cup sugar
- 1/2 teaspoon vanilla extract

For crust, in a large bowl, cream butter and sugar until light and fluffy. Beat in vanilla. Gradually add the flour, oats and salt; mix well. Press over the bottom and sides of a 9-in. pie plate. Cover and refrigerate.

Combine rhubarb and water in a saucepan. Bring to a boil, stirring constantly. Combine the sugar, flour and salt; add to the rhubarb mixture. Cook and stir over medium-high heat until thickened and bubbly. Reduce heat; cook and stir 2 minutes longer. Remove from the heat. Stir a small amount of hot filling into egg yolks; return all to pan, stirring constantly. Bring to a gentle boil; cook and stir 2 minutes longer. Remove from the heat. Cool slightly.

Pour filling into crust. Bake at 375° for 25-30 minutes.

In a large bowl, beat egg whites and salt on medium speed until soft peaks form. Gradually beat in sugar, 1 tablespoon at a time, on high until stiff, glossy peaks form and sugar is dissolved. Beat in vanilla. Spread evenly over hot filling, sealing edges to crust. Bake at

350° for 12-15 minutes or until the meringue is golden brown. Cool on a wire rack for 1 hour. Refrigerate for at least 3 hours before serving. Store leftovers in the refrigerator. **yield: 6-8 servings.**

editor's note: If using frozen rhubarb, measure rhubarb while still frozen, then thaw completely. Drain in a colander, but do not press liquid out.

summer berry pie

Judi Messina • Coeur d'Alene, Idaho
My mom puts luscious fresh blueberries, strawberries and raspberries to great use in this cool, refreshing pie. It's a super dessert on a hot day.

- 1-1/2 cups sugar
- 6 tablespoons cornstarch
- 3 cups cold water
- 2 packages (3 ounces *each*) raspberry *or* strawberry gelatin
- 2 cups fresh blueberries
- 2 cups sliced fresh strawberries
- 2 cups fresh raspberries
- 2 graham cracker crusts (9 inches)
- 4 cups whipped topping

Fresh mint and additional sliced strawberries

In a large saucepan, combine the sugar, cornstarch and water until smooth. Bring to a boil; cook and stir for 2 minutes or until thickened. Remove from the heat. Stir in gelatin until dissolved. Refrigerate for 15-20 minutes or until mixture begins to thicken.

Stir in the berries. Pour into crusts and chill until set. Garnish with whipped topping, mint and strawberries. **yield: 2 pies (6-8 servings each).**

summer berry pie

rustic fruit tart

rustic fruit tart

Naomi Olson • Hamilton, Michigan

My husband and I love pie, but we can't eat a whole 9-inch pie by ourselves. So I make these easy tarts using rhubarb and fruit from our red raspberry bushes. Sometimes I substitute apples, peaches or our homegrown blueberries for the rhubarb.

  1 **cup all-purpose flour**
1/2 **teaspoon salt**
1/4 **cup canola oil**
  2 **tablespoons milk**
  1 **cup diced fresh *or* frozen rhubarb, thawed**
  1 **cup fresh *or* frozen raspberries, thawed**
1/2 **cup sugar**
  2 **tablespoons quick-cooking tapioca**
GLAZE:
  6 **tablespoons confectioners' sugar**
  1 **teaspoon water**
1/8 **teaspoon almond extract**

In a large bowl, combine flour and salt. Add oil and milk, tossing with a fork until mixture forms a ball. Shape dough into a disk; wrap in plastic wrap. Refrigerate for at least 1 hour.

In another bowl, combine the rhubarb, raspberries, sugar and tapioca; let stand for 15 minutes. Unwrap dough and place on a parchment-lined baking sheet. Cover with waxed paper and roll the dough into an 11-in. circle. Discard waxed paper.

Spoon fruit mixture into the center of dough to within 2 in. of the edges. Fold edges of dough over fruit, leaving center uncovered. Bake at 400° for 25-30 minutes or until crust is golden brown and filling is bubbly. Remove to a wire rack. Combine the glaze ingredients until smooth. Drizzle over warm tart. **yield: 2 servings.**

editor's note: If using frozen rhubarb, measure rhubarb while still frozen, then thaw completely. Drain in a colander, but do not press liquid out.

star-studded blueberry pie

Nancy Barker • Silverton, Oregon
Family and friends say this pleasing pie is better than a popular one served at a local restaurant. If desired, use gooseberries for half of the blueberries.

  4 **cups fresh *or* frozen blueberries**
  1 **cup sugar**
1/4 **cup quick-cooking tapioca**
  1 **tablespoon lemon juice**
1/4 **teaspoon salt**
Pastry for double-crust pie (9 inches)
  2 **tablespoons butter**

In a large bowl, combine the blueberries, sugar, tapioca, lemon juice and salt; toss gently. Let stand for 15 minutes. Line a 9-in. pie plate with bottom pastry; add filling. Dot with butter; flute edges.

Cover edges loosely with foil. Bake at 400° for 25 minutes. Remove foil; bake 20-25 minutes longer or until set. Cool on a wire rack.

From remaining pastry, cut out 15 large stars with a 2-in. cookie cutter and 15 small stars with a 1/2-in. cookie cutter. Place on an ungreased baking sheet. Bake at 350° for 5-10 minutes or until golden brown. Remove to wire racks to cool. Randomly place stars over cooled pie. **yield: 8 servings.**

star-studded blueberry pie

Taste of Home
Test Kitchen
Greendale, Wisconsin
*Apricot and chocolate are
pleasing partners in this
elegant dessert created by
our home economists.
The tart doesn't contain
flour, so it's appropriate
for people watching their
carbohydrates.*

flourless apricot pecan tart

12	ounces dried apricots, chopped
1	cup water
6	tablespoons sugar
1	tablespoon minced fresh gingerroot
1	tablespoon lemon juice
1	teaspoon grated lemon peel

CRUST:

1	tablespoon matzo meal
4	cups pecan halves, toasted
1-1/2	cups sugar
1/2	teaspoon ground ginger
1/4	teaspoon salt
2	eggs
4	squares (1 ounce *each*) semisweet chocolate

GARNISH:

2	squares (1 ounce *each*) semisweet chocolate
1/2	cup pecan halves

Dried apricots

In a heavy saucepan, combine the apricots, water, sugar, gingerroot, lemon juice and peel; bring to a boil. Reduce heat; cover and simmer for 30-35 minutes or until apricots are tender. Uncover; simmer 5-10 minutes longer or until thickened and liquid is absorbed. Transfer to a food processor; cover and pulse five times or until mixture is smooth and thickened. Pour into a bowl; cool.

Trace the removable bottom of an 11-in. tart pan on waxed paper; set aside. Grease tart pan; dust with matzo meal and set aside.

In a food processor, combine the pecans, sugar, ginger and salt; cover and process until pecans are finely ground. Add eggs; cover and process until mixture forms a moist ball. Place half of the dough in a bowl; cover and refrigerate. Press remaining dough over the bottom and up the sides of prepared pan. Bake at 350° for 12-15 minutes or until crust is puffed and lightly browned. Press bottom of crust lightly to flatten if necessary. Cool on a wire rack.

In a microwave, melt chocolate; stir until smooth. Spread over crust. Chill for 10 minutes or until set. Spread apricot filling over chocolate. Press remaining dough over waxed paper circle. Invert dough over filling; carefully peel off waxed paper and discard. Press edges of dough to edge of tart pan to seal.

Bake at 350° for 35-40 minutes or until lightly browned and dry to the touch. Cool completely in pan on a wire rack. Cover with foil and let stand overnight.

For garnish, melt chocolate; stir until smooth. Drizzle 2 tablespoons over tart. Dip pecans halfway in remaining chocolate. Garnish tart with dipped pecans and dried apricots. **yield: 12-14 servings.**

stacked high

raspberry-cream chocolate torte, p. 30

Layer after layer of tender, fluffy cakes, skyscraper tortes decorated in style, fresh fruit and cream piled high in towering trifles…these soaring delights raise the bar when it comes to dessert! Serve any one of the grand champions in this chapter, and you are sure to earn rave reviews for reaching new heights in dessert excellence.

blackberry custard torte

blackberry custard torte

Ann Fox • Austin, Texas
Sour cream gives the custard an interesting flavor twist in this outstanding dessert piled high with blackberries.

    1   cup all-purpose flour
    1/2 cup sugar
    1-1/2 teaspoons baking powder
    1/2 cup cold butter
    1   egg
FILLING:
    3   egg yolks
    2   cups (16 ounces) sour cream
    1/2 cup sugar
    1/4 teaspoon vanilla extract
    4   cups fresh *or* frozen blackberries, drained, *divided*
Whipped cream

In a small bowl, combine the flour, sugar and baking powder; cut in butter until crumbly. Stir in egg until dough forms a ball. Press onto the bottom and 2 in. up the sides of an ungreased 9-in. springform pan.

For filling, in another small bowl, beat the egg yolks, sour cream, sugar and vanilla just until combined. Sprinkle 2 cups blackberries over crust. Carefully pour sour cream mixture over berries. Place the pan on a baking sheet.

Bake at 325° for 1-1/2 hours or until center is almost set. Cool on a wire rack (center will fall).

Remove sides of pan. Top with whipped cream and remaining blackberries. Refrigerate any leftovers. **yield: 12-14 servings.**

editor's note: This dessert is best eaten the same day it's prepared.

sweetheart trifle

Lorie Cooper • Chatham, Ontario
If you're a peanut butter and chocolate lover, this heavenly trifle is for you. It's a hit every time I serve it, and I always get requests for the recipe.

    1   package (18-1/4 ounces) chocolate cake mix
    1   package (10 ounces) peanut butter chips
4-1/4   cups cold milk, *divided*
    1/2 cup heavy whipping cream
    1/4 teaspoon vanilla extract
    2   packages (5.9 ounces *each*) instant chocolate pudding mix
    1   carton (12 ounces) frozen whipped topping, thawed
    4   Nestlé Crunch candy bars (1.55 ounces *each*), crumbled

Prepare cake mix according to package directions. Pour the batter into a greased 13-in. x 9-in. baking pan.

Bake at 350° for 30-35 minutes or until a toothpick inserted near the center comes out clean. Cool on a wire rack.

In a heavy saucepan, combine chips, 1/4 cup milk and cream. Cook and stir over low heat until chips are melted. Remove from the heat; stir in vanilla. Cool to room temperature. In a large bowl, whisk the milk and pudding mixes for 2 minutes. Let stand for 2 minutes or until soft-set.

To assemble, crumble half of the cake into a 4-qt. trifle bowl or large bowl. Layer half of the peanut butter sauce, pudding, whipped topping and candy bars; repeat layers. Cover and refrigerate for at least 3 hours before serving. **yield: 12-15 servings.**

sweetheart trifle

genoise with fruit & cream filling

DESSERT *Tip*

A Genoise cake is a light sponge cake that does not use any chemical leavening during baking. Instead, it is the air suspended in the batter during mixing that gives volume to the cake. Although named after the city of Genoa in Italy, this method was adapted by the French and is now used to make elegant pastries including petits fours, layered cakes and cake rolls.

*Taste of Home
Test Kitchen
Greendale, Wisconsin*
Sweet syrup soaks into the tender layers of this sponge cake topped with sweetened cream and fresh berries.

genoise with fruit & cream filling

6	eggs, lightly beaten
1	cup sugar
1	teaspoon grated lemon peel
1	teaspoon lemon extract
1	cup all-purpose flour
1/2	cup butter, melted and cooled

SUGAR SYRUP:

3	tablespoons boiling water
2	tablespoons sugar
1/4	cup cold water
1-1/2	teaspoons lemon extract

FILLING:

1	cup heavy whipping cream
1/2	cup confectioners' sugar
1	teaspoon vanilla extract, optional
3	cups mixed fresh berries

Line two greased 9-in. round baking pans with waxed paper and grease the paper; set aside. In a large heat-proof bowl, combine eggs and sugar; place over a large saucepan filled with 1-2 in. of simmering water. Heat over low heat, stirring occasionally, until mixture reaches 110°, about 8-10 minutes.

Remove from the heat; add lemon peel and extract. With a hand mixer, beat on high speed until mixture is lemon-colored and more than doubles in volume. Fold in flour, 1/4 cup at a time. Gently fold in butter. Spread into prepared pans.

Bake at 350° for 25-30 minutes or until a toothpick inserted near the center comes out clean. Cool for 10 minutes before removing from pans to wire racks to cool completely.

In a small bowl, combine boiling water and sugar; stir until sugar is dissolved. Stir in cold water and extract. Using a fork, evenly poke 1/2-in.-deep holes in each cake. Spoon sugar syrup over cake surface.

In a small bowl, beat cream until it begins to thicken. Add sugar and vanilla if desired; beat until soft peaks form.

Place one cake on a serving platter; spread with half of the whipped cream and top with half of the berries. Repeat layers. Store in the refrigerator. **yield: 10-12 servings.**

peanut butter apple dessert

Kim Spencer • Hickman, Nebraska

My mom, who's known in our community for her cooking, shared the recipe for this yummy and impressive dessert. It's very popular with my husband. In fact, he made it for his men's Bible study group and ended up giving out the recipe!

1-1/2	cups graham cracker crumbs (about 24 squares)
1/2	cup packed brown sugar
1/2	cup plus 1/3 cup peanut butter, *divided*
1/4	cup butter, melted
1	package (8 ounces) cream cheese, softened
3/4	cup sugar
1	carton (16 ounces) frozen whipped topping, thawed
2	cans (21 ounces *each*) apple pie filling
3/4	cup confectioners' sugar
1	teaspoon ground cinnamon

In a large bowl, combine the graham cracker crumbs, brown sugar, 1/2 cup peanut butter and butter; spoon half into a 3-qt. bowl.

In a large bowl, beat the cream cheese and sugar until smooth; fold in whipped topping. Spread half over crumb mixture in the bowl. Top with one can of apple pie filling.

Combine the confectioners' sugar, cinnamon and the remaining peanut butter until crumbly; sprinkle half over pie filling. Repeat layers. Refrigerate until serving. **yield: about 20 servings.**

peanut butter apple dessert

orange chocolate torte

orange chocolate torte

Georgiana Hagman • Louisville, Kentucky

This eye-catching dessert takes the cake at any holiday gathering. Chocolate truffles atop this three-layer cake are a fantastic finishing touch.

2	cups (12 ounces) semisweet chocolate chips
6	tablespoons butter, cubed
4	egg yolks
6	tablespoons confectioners' sugar
1/4	cup chocolate sprinkles *or* ground pecans

CAKE:

1	cup butter, softened
2-1/2	cups sugar
4	eggs
1-1/2	teaspoons orange extract
2-1/4	cups all-purpose flour
1	cup baking cocoa
2	teaspoons baking powder
1/2	teaspoon baking soda
1/2	teaspoon salt
2	cups water

FROSTING:

1	cup butter, cubed
1	cup (6 ounces) semisweet chocolate chips
1/3	cup plus 7 to 8 tablespoons milk, *divided*
1	teaspoon orange extract
2-3/4	cups sifted confectioners' sugar

Chocolate sprinkles

In a large heavy saucepan, stir chocolate chips and butter until melted. In a small bowl, beat egg yolks until lemon-colored. Gradually stir in warm chocolate mixture; return all to the pan. Cook and stir over medium heat until mixture reaches 160°.

Remove from the heat. Stir in confectioners' sugar until blended. Place 1/2 cup in a small bowl; pour remaining chocolate mixture into a small bowl for filling. Cover each bowl with a paper towel. Let stand for up to 1 hour or until soft-set.

For truffles, roll the 1/2-cup portion into 12 balls. Roll in sprinkles or pecans. Cover and refrigerate until serving.

In a large bowl, cream butter and sugar until light and fluffy. Add eggs, one at a time, beating well after each addition. Beat in extract. Combine flour, cocoa, baking powder, baking soda and salt; gradually add to creamed mixture alternately with water.

Pour into three greased and floured 9-in. round baking pans. Bake at 350° for 25-30 minutes or until a toothpick inserted near the center comes out clean. Cool for 10 minutes; remove cakes from pans to wire racks to cool completely.

For frosting, in a microwave-safe bowl, combine the butter, chocolate chips and 1/3 cup milk; microwave until melted. Whisk in extract until smooth. Gradually whisk in confectioners' sugar.

Transfer to a large bowl. Place in a large bowl of ice water. With a hand mixer, beat on medium speed until stiff peaks form, about 7 minutes; set aside.

For filling, gradually add enough of the remaining milk to reserved chocolate mixture, beating until it achieves spreading consistency.

Place one cake layer on a serving plate; spread with half of the filling. Repeat layers. Spread 2-2/3 cups frosting over top and sides of cake. Using a #195 star tip, pipe the remaining frosting into 12 rosettes on top of cake. Place a truffle on each rosette. Lightly press chocolate sprinkles onto sides of cake. Store in the refrigerator. **yield: 12 servings.**

angel food delight

Beth Stephas • Eagle Grove, Iowa
Whip up this delicious cake for a showstopping ending to any meal. With only four ingredients, it's so simple to prepare, yet looks like you spent hours fussing.

> 1 carton (8 ounces) frozen whipped topping, thawed
> 1 jar (16 ounces) chocolate fudge sauce
> 1 prepared angel food cake (16 ounces)
> 3/4 cup English toffee bits

In a large bowl, fold whipped topping into chocolate sauce just until blended. Split cake horizontally into three layers; place one layer on a serving plate. Spread with a fourth of the topping mixture and a fourth of the toffee bits. Repeat layers. Top with remaining cake layer.

Frost the top and sides with remaining topping mixture; sprinkle with remaining toffee bits. Cover and refrigerate for 4 hours. Refrigerate leftovers. **yield: 8-10 servings.**

raspberry trifle

Marcy Cella • L'Anse, Michigan
Beautiful and luscious, this trifle is an impressive way to use fresh raspberries.

> 1 package (16 ounces) pound cake, cut into 18 slices *or* 2 packages (3 ounces *each*) ladyfingers
> 2 packages (3.4 ounces *each*) instant vanilla pudding mix
> 1 jar (18 ounces) raspberry jam
> 1-1/2 pints fresh raspberries
> **Whipped cream and fresh raspberries, for garnish**

Arrange one-third of sliced cake in the bottom of a trifle dish or large decorative bowl.

Prepare pudding according to package directions. Place one-third more cake pieces around inside of bowl, using half of pudding to hold them in place.

Gently stir together jam and raspberries; spoon half over pudding. Cover with remaining cake pieces. Layer remaining pudding and raspberry mixture. Chill. Garnish with whipped cream and fresh raspberries. **yield: 8-10 servings.**

raspberry trifle

strawberry towers

Nancy Donato • Uniontown, Ohio

A few years ago, I hosted a Valentine's Day party with a heart theme. This stunning grand finale received rave reviews.

          1   sheet frozen puff pastry, thawed
          1   tablespoon cinnamon-sugar
      1/4   cup semisweet chocolate chips
      1/4   teaspoon shortening
      3/4   cup heavy whipping cream
          1   tablespoon sugar
      1/4   teaspoon clear vanilla extract
          1   cup sliced fresh strawberries

On a lightly floured surface, roll pastry sheet into a 14-in. x 10-in. rectangle. Using three different sizes of heart-shaped cookie cutters (3-1/2 in., 3 in. and 1 in.), cut out 12 hearts, four of each size (discard scraps).

Place 2 in. apart on a greased baking sheet. Sprinkle with cinnamon-sugar. Bake at 400° for 8-10 minutes or until golden brown; remove smallest hearts to a wire rack. Bake medium and large hearts 2 minutes longer; remove to a wire rack.

In a small microwave-safe bowl, melt chocolate chips and shortening; stir until smooth. Transfer mixture to a small resealable plastic bag; cut a small hole in a corner of the bag. In a small bowl, beat cream until it begins to thicken. Add sugar and vanilla; beat until stiff peaks form.

To assemble, place large pastry hearts on dessert plates; top with a third of the whipped cream and half of the strawberries. Drizzle with chocolate. Top with

medium hearts, another third of the whipped cream and remaining strawberries. Drizzle with chocolate. Dollop with remaining whipped cream. Pipe chocolate around edge of small hearts; insert into whipped cream at top of tower. **yield: 4 servings.**

white chocolate torte

Norma Van Devander • Calais, Maine

Looking for a change from heavy, chocolatly desserts? Try this white chocolate cake! It's wonderfully moist and slices well.

          1   cup butter, softened
          2   cups sugar
          4   squares (1 ounce *each*) white baking
              chocolate, melted and cooled
          4   eggs
     1-1/2   teaspoons clear vanilla extract
          3   cups all-purpose flour
          1   teaspoon baking soda
          1   cup buttermilk
      1/2   cup water
      1/2   cup chopped pecans, toasted
FROSTING:
          2   packages (one 8 ounces, one 3 ounces) cream
              cheese, softened
      1/3   cup butter, softened
          4   squares (1 ounce *each*) white baking
              chocolate, melted and cooled
     1-1/2   teaspoons clear vanilla extract
     6-1/2   cups confectioners' sugar
Chocolate curls

Line three greased 9-in. round baking pans with waxed paper and grease the paper; set aside. In a large bowl, cream butter and sugar until light and fluffy. Beat in chocolate. Add eggs, one at a time, beating well after each. Beat in vanilla. Combine flour and baking soda; gradually add to creamed mixture alternately with buttermilk and water, beating well after each addition. Fold in pecans. Pour batter into prepared pans.

Bake at 350° for 23-27 minutes or until a toothpick inserted near the center comes out clean. Cool for 10 minutes before removing from pans to wire racks; discard waxed paper.

For frosting, in a large bowl, beat cream cheese and butter until fluffy. Beat in chocolate and vanilla. Gradually add confectioners' sugar until smooth. Spread frosting between layers and over top and sides of cake. Garnish with chocolate curls. Store in the refrigerator. **yield: 14-16 servings.**

banana macaroon trifle

Barbara Keith • Faucett, Missouri
A chewy homemade macaroon mixture replaces traditional cake cubes usually called for in trifles. No time to bake? Use store-bought macaroons instead.

- 2 **tablespoons butter, softened**
- 1 **cup sugar**
- 1 **egg**
- 1 **teaspoon vanilla extract**
- 2 **tablespoons all-purpose flour**
- 1/2 **cup old-fashioned oats**
- 1 **teaspoon baking powder**
- 1/4 **cup milk**
- 1 **cup flaked coconut**
- 3 **to 4 small firm bananas, sliced**
- 1 **tablespoon pineapple juice**
- 1 **carton (12 ounces) frozen whipped topping, thawed**

In a large bowl, cream butter and sugar until light and fluffy. Beat in egg and vanilla. Combine the flour, oats and baking powder; add to creamed mixture alternately with milk, beating well after each addition (mixture will appear curdled). Stir in coconut.

Spread in a well-greased 13-in. x 9-in. baking pan. Bake at 325° for 25-30 minutes or until edges are golden brown. Cool completely; crumble. Set aside 1/4 cup for topping.

Just before serving, toss bananas with pineapple juice. In a 2-1/2-qt. serving bowl, layer a third of the

easy boston cream cake

macaroon crumbs, whipped topping and bananas. Repeat layers twice. Sprinkle with reserved crumbs. **yield: 8-10 servings.**

easy boston cream cake

Taste of Home Test Kitchen • Greendale, Wisconsin
Why make a Boston cream pie from scratch when this cake version is so simple? Preparing the pudding with half-and-half cream instead of milk gives this grand dessert an added richness that's hard to beat.

- 1-1/2 **cups cold half-and-half cream**
- 1 **package (3.4 ounces) instant vanilla pudding mix**
- 1 **loaf (10-3/4 ounces) frozen pound cake, thawed**
- 3/4 **cup confectioners' sugar**
- 2 **tablespoons baking cocoa**
- 4 **to 5 teaspoons hot water**

In a large bowl, whisk together cream and pudding mix for 2 minutes. Let stand for 2 minutes or until soft-set.

Cut cake into three horizontal layers. Place bottom layer on a serving plate; top with half of the pudding. Repeat layers. Top with third cake layer.

In a small bowl, combine the confectioners' sugar, cocoa and enough water to reach desired spreading consistency. Spread over top of cake, letting glaze drizzle down sides. **yield: 4-6 servings.**

Mary Beth Jung
Hendersonville,
North Carolina

This spectacular torte looks and tastes like it came from a European bakery. Although it takes some time to make, each step is actually quite easy.

raspberry-cream chocolate torte

2/3 **cup butter, softened**
1 **cup sugar**
3 **eggs**
2 **teaspoons vanilla extract**
2 **cups all-purpose flour**
3/4 **cup baking cocoa**
1-1/2 **teaspoons baking powder**
1/2 **teaspoon baking soda**
1-1/3 **cups milk**
FILLING:
1 **package (10 ounces) frozen unsweetened raspberries, thawed**
1 **envelope unflavored gelatin**
1 **cup heavy whipping cream**
1/4 **cup confectioners' sugar**
1/2 **teaspoon vanilla extract**
GANACHE:
1/2 **cup semisweet chocolate chips**
3 **tablespoons heavy whipping cream**

In a large bowl, cream butter and sugar until light and fluffy. Beat in eggs and vanilla. Combine the flour, cocoa, baking powder and soda; gradually add to creamed mixture alternately with milk, beating well after each addition.

Line a greased 15-in. x 10-in. x 1-in. baking pan with waxed paper; grease the paper. Spread batter evenly into pan. Bake at 350° for 15-20 minutes or until cake springs back when lightly touched in center. Cool for 10 minutes before removing from pan to a wire rack; carefully remove paper. Cool completely.

For filling, puree raspberries in a food processor. Strain, reserving juice and discarding seeds. Place juice in a small saucepan. Sprinkle with gelatin; let stand for 1 minute. Cook and stir over low heat until gelatin is completely dissolved. Cool to room temperature.

In a small bowl, beat cream until it begins to thicken. Add confectioners' sugar and vanilla; beat until stiff peaks form. Gently fold into the raspberry mixture.

Trim edges from cake. Cut into four 7-1/2-in. x 4-1/2-in. rectangles. Place one rectangle on a serving platter; spread with a third of the filling. Repeat layers twice. Top with remaining rectangle.

For ganache, place chocolate chips and cream in a small saucepan. Cook and stir over low heat until chocolate is melted. Cool until thickened, about 10 minutes. Spread over torte. Refrigerate for 2 hours before serving. **yield: 8-10 servings.**

coconut chocolate trifle

Donna Cline • Pensacola, Florida

You don't even need to taste this luscious dessert—just one look and you'll say "wow!" Apricot preserves add a fruity touch to the pleasing pairing of chocolate and toasted coconut in this easy-to-assemble trifle.

- 1 loaf (10-3/4 ounces) frozen pound cake, thawed
- 1/3 cup apricot preserves
- 1/3 cup plus 2 tablespoons orange juice, *divided*
- 1 package (4 ounces) German sweet chocolate
- 1-1/4 cups flaked coconut, toasted, *divided*
- 1-3/4 cups cold milk
- 1 cup half-and-half cream
- 1 package (5.9 ounces) instant chocolate pudding mix

Trim crust from top, sides and bottom of cake. Cut cake into 16 slices. Spread preserves over eight slices; top with remaining cake. Cut into 1-in. cubes.

Place in a 2-qt. serving bowl; drizzle with 1/3 cup orange juice. Chop chocolate; set aside 2 tablespoons for garnish. Sprinkle remaining chocolate and 1 cup coconut over cake.

In a large bowl, combine the milk, cream, pudding mix and remaining orange juice; beat on low for 2 minutes. Spoon over cake. Sprinkle with remaining coconut and reserved chocolate. Refrigerate for at least 4 hours before serving. **yield: 10-14 servings.**

chocolate chiffon valentine cake

Pat Eastman • Provo, Utah

I first made this lovely, lightly textured cake for my husband on Valentine's Day more than 25 years ago, but it suits any special occasion. For an alternative, decorate the top of this tall cake with chocolate kisses in place of the strawberries.

- 4 eggs, *separated*
- 1/2 cup baking cocoa
- 1/2 cup hot water
- 3/4 cup all-purpose flour
- 1-1/4 cups sugar, *divided*
- 3/4 teaspoon baking soda
- 1/2 teaspoon salt
- 1/4 cup canola oil
- 1 teaspoon vanilla extract
- 1/4 teaspoon cream of tartar

FROSTING:
- 1-1/2 cups heavy whipping cream
- 1/4 cup confectioners' sugar
- 15 small fresh strawberries, halved

Fresh mint, optional

Let egg whites stand at room temperature for 30 minutes. Line two greased 9-in. heart-shaped pans with waxed paper and grease the paper; set aside. In a small bowl, combine cocoa and water until smooth; cool.

In a large bowl, combine the flour, 1 cup sugar, baking soda and salt. In another bowl, whisk the egg yolks, oil, vanilla and cocoa mixture. Add to dry ingredients; beat until well blended.

In a small bowl, beat egg whites and cream of tartar until soft peaks form. Gradually add the remaining sugar, 1 tablespoon at a time, beating until stiff peaks form; fold into chocolate mixture.

Pour into prepared pans. Bake at 350° for 18-20 minutes or until top springs back when lightly touched. Cool for 10 minutes before removing from pans to wire racks to cool completely; carefully remove waxed paper.

In a large bowl, beat cream until it begins to thicken. Add confectioners' sugar until stiff peaks form; reserving 1-1/2 cups. Spread remaining frosting between layers and over top and sides of cake.

Spoon reserved frosting into a pastry bag with a star tip. Pipe a decorative lattice design on cake top and sides. Garnish with strawberries and mint if desired. Refrigerate until serving. **yield: 12 servings.**

chocolate chiffon valentine cake

chocolate strawberry torte

until blended. Add the eggs, one at a time, beating well after each addition. Beat in vanilla. Combine the flour, baking soda and salt; gradually add to the chocolate mixture alternately with water, beating well after each addition.

Pour into two greased and floured 9-in. round baking pans. Bake at 350° for 28-33 minutes or until a toothpick inserted near the center comes out clean. Cool for 10 minutes before removing from pans to wire racks.

In a large bowl, combine filling ingredients; set aside. For glaze, in a microwave, melt chocolate and butter; stir until smooth. Stir in confectioners' sugar, water and vanilla until smooth. Cool slightly.

Place one cake layer on a serving plate. Spread with half of the whipped topping; drizzle with half of the glaze. Top with half of the filling. Repeat layers. Store in the refrigerator. **yield: 10-12 servings.**

chocolate strawberry torte

Paula Magnus • Republic, Washington
This towering torte combines the mouth-watering flavors of chocolate and strawberries. A drizzle of glaze on top adds the crowning touch to this dazzling dessert.

5	squares (1 ounce *each*) semisweet chocolate
3/4	cup butter, cubed
1-1/2	cups sugar
3	eggs
2	teaspoons vanilla extract
2-1/2	cups all-purpose flour
1	teaspoon baking soda
1/4	teaspoon salt
1-1/2	cups water

STRAWBERRY FILLING:

4	cups sliced fresh strawberries
2	tablespoons sugar
1	teaspoon vanilla extract

GLAZE:

3	squares (1 ounce *each*) semisweet chocolate
1	tablespoon butter
1	cup confectioners' sugar
3	tablespoons water
1/2	teaspoon vanilla extract
1	carton (8 ounces) frozen whipped topping, thawed

In a microwave, melt chocolate and butter; stir until smooth. Cool. Transfer to a large bowl; beating sugar

cherry cream trifle

Juanita Davis • Martin, Tennessee
Not only is this dessert cool and creamy, it's a conversation piece when presented in a punch bowl!

1	package (18-1/4 ounces) yellow cake mix
2	packages (3.4 ounces *each*) instant vanilla pudding mix
2	cans (21 ounces *each*) cherry pie filling
2	cans (20 ounces *each*) crushed pineapple, drained
2	cartons (16 ounces *each*) frozen whipped topping, thawed
2	cups chopped pecans

cherry cream trifle

Prepare and bake cake according to package directions for a 13-in. x 9-in. pan. Cool on a wire rack. Meanwhile, prepare pudding according to package directions.

Cut cake into 1-1/2-in. cubes; place a third of the cubes in an 8-qt. punch bowl. Top with a third of the pie filling, pineapple, pudding, whipped topping and pecans; repeat layers twice. Cover and refrigerate until serving. **yield: 25-30 servings.**

chocolate angel food cake

Mary Ann Iverson • Woodville, Wisconsin
Chocolate lovers will go crazy for this impressive angel food cake. Whenever I bring it to church bake sales, it goes before I can get it on the table!

1-1/2 cups egg whites (about 10)
  3/4 cup cake flour
1-1/2 cups plus 2 tablespoons sugar, *divided*
  1/4 cup baking cocoa
1-1/2 teaspoons cream of tartar
1-1/2 teaspoons vanilla extract
  1/4 teaspoon salt
CHOCOLATE FLUFF FROSTING:
    2 cups heavy whipping cream
    1 cup sifted confectioners' sugar
  1/2 cup baking cocoa
Dash salt

Place egg whites in a large bowl; let stand at room temperature for 30 minutes. Sift the flour, 3/4 cup plus 2 tablespoons sugar and cocoa three times. Set aside.

Add cream of tartar, vanilla and salt to egg whites; beat on medium speed until soft peaks form. Gradually add sugar, about 2 tablespoons at a time, beating on high until stiff, glossy peaks form and sugar is dissolved. Gradually fold in flour mixture, about 1/2 cup at a time. Mixture will be thick.

Gently spoon into an ungreased 10-in. tube pan. Cut through the batter with a knife to remove air pockets. Bake on the lowest oven rack at 350° for 40-45 minutes or until lightly browned and entire top appears dry. Immediately invert pan; cool completely, about 1 hour.

Run a knife around side and center tube of pan. Remove cake to a serving plate.

For frosting, in a large bowl, beat cream until it begins to thicken. Add the sugar, cocoa and salt; beat until stiff peaks form. Frost the top and sides of the cake. **yield: 12 servings.**

blueberry graham dessert

blueberry graham dessert

Taste of Home Test Kitchen • Greendale, Wisconsin
When you're short on time but long for cheesecake, try this fruity dessert. Ricotta and cream cheeses give every bite the flavor of cheesecake but without the fuss. Instead of making individual servings, layer the ingredients in a large glass serving bowl.

  3/4 cup graham cracker crumbs (about
       12 squares)
  1/4 cup chopped walnuts
    2 tablespoons sugar
  1/4 teaspoon ground cinnamon
    2 tablespoons butter
    1 package (3 ounces) cream cheese, softened
  1/3 cup confectioners' sugar
  1/2 cup ricotta cheese
    2 teaspoons lemon juice
    4 cups fresh blueberries
Whipped cream, optional

In a large bowl, combine the cracker crumbs, walnuts, sugar and cinnamon. Stir in butter; set aside. In a large bowl, beat cream cheese and confectioners' sugar until smooth. Beat in ricotta cheese and lemon juice.

Place 1/2 cup blueberries each in four dessert dishes. Top with cream cheese mixture, crumbs and remaining blueberries. Garnish with whipped cream if desired. Refrigerate until serving. **yield: 4 servings.**

berry tiramisu cake

Diane Way • Harrisburg, Pennsylvania

I love traditional tiramisu but my husband isn't crazy over the coffee flavor. So I got a little creative, leaving out the mocha and adding fresh berries. The result was this sky-high cake!

    4   cups assorted fresh berries
    1   cup sugar
    1   tablespoon lemon juice
    2   teaspoons cornstarch
CAKE:
1-1/2   cups all-purpose flour
    1   cup plus 2 tablespoons sugar, *divided*
    2   teaspoons baking powder
  1/2   teaspoon salt
    4   eggs, *separated*
  1/2   cup water
  1/3   cup canola oil
CREAM FILLING:
    1   package (8 ounces) cream cheese, softened
  1/2   cup confectioners' sugar
    2   cups heavy whipping cream, whipped

In a large bowl, combine the berries, sugar and lemon juice. Cover and refrigerate for 1 hour. Gently press berries; drain, reserving juice. Set berries aside.

In a large saucepan, combine cornstarch and reserved juice until smooth. Bring to a boil; cook and stir for 1-2 minutes or until thickened. Cool completely.

berry tiramisu cake

In a large bowl, combine the flour, 1 cup sugar, baking powder and salt. Whisk egg yolks, water and oil; add to dry ingredients, beating until smooth.

In another bowl, beat egg whites on medium speed until soft peaks form. Gradually add remaining sugar, beating on high until stiff peaks form; fold into batter. Spread into an ungreased 9-in. springform pan.

Bake at 325° for 30-38 minutes or until cake springs back when lightly touched. Cool for 10 minutes; remove from pan and cool on a wire rack. Meanwhile, in a large bowl, beat cream cheese and confectioners' sugar until smooth. Fold in whipped cream; set aside.

Cut cake horizontally into three layers. Place bottom layer on a serving plate; spread with a third of the filling. Top with a third of the berries; drizzle with 1/4 cup berry syrup. Repeat layers twice, drizzling with remaining syrup. Refrigerate for at least 2 hours before serving. **yield: 12 servings.**

cherry cream torte

Mary Anne McWhirter • Pearland, Texas

When you set this gorgeous dessert on the table, your guests will sing your praises. You're the only one who has to know how simple it is to prepare.

    2   packages (3 ounces *each*) ladyfingers
    2   tablespoons white grape *or* apple juice
    1   package (8 ounces) cream cheese, softened
  2/3   cup sugar
    1   teaspoon almond extract, *divided*
    2   cups whipping cream, whipped
    1   can (21 ounces) cherry pie filling
Toasted sliced almonds and additional whipped
    cream, optional

Split ladyfingers lengthwise; brush with juice. Place a layer of ladyfingers around the sides and over the bottom of a lightly greased 9-in. springform pan.

In a large bowl, beat cream cheese until smooth; add sugar and 1/2 teaspoon extract. Beat on medium for 1 minute. Fold in whipped cream. Spread half over crust.

Arrange remaining ladyfingers in a spoke-like fashion. Spread evenly with the remaining cream cheese mixture. Cover and chill overnight.

Combine the pie filling and remaining extract; spread over the cream cheese layer. Refrigerate for at least 2 hours. To serve, remove sides of pan. Garnish with sliced almonds and whipped cream if desired. **yield: 16-18 servings.**

edna's ho ho cake

edna's ho ho cake

Edna Miller • Mount Hope, Ohio
Whenever I make this cake, I get rave reviews. With a creamy filling and glossy chocolate glaze, this scrumptious confection beats any ordinary ho ho.

     2   **prepared 9-in. round chocolate cakes**
FILLING:
     2   **tablespoons all-purpose flour**
     1   **cup milk**
   2/3   **cup sugar, *divided***
   2/3   **cup shortening**
   1/3   **cup butter, softened**
   3/4   **teaspoon vanilla extract**
Pinch salt
GLAZE:
   1/4   **cup butter, cubed**
   1/4   **cup baking cocoa**
   3/4   **cup confectioners' sugar**
     2   **to 4 tablespoons milk**

For filling, in a small saucepan, combine flour and milk until smooth; stir in 1/4 cup sugar. Bring to a boil over medium heat; cook and stir for 2 minutes or until thickened. Transfer to a large bowl; cool. Beat in the shortening, butter, vanilla, salt and remaining sugar until smooth. Spread between cake layers.

For glaze, melt butter and cocoa in a small saucepan. Whisk in confectioners' sugar and enough milk to achieve a drizzling consistency. Drizzle over the top of the cake, allowing some to drape down the sides. **yield: 12-16 servings.**

yum-yum cake

Teresa Marchese • New Berlin, Wisconsin
This cake has been a family favorite for years. Great for any occasion, this is one dessert that truly lives up to its name!

 1-1/2   **cups cold milk**
     1   **package (3.4 ounces) instant vanilla pudding mix**
     1   **package (18-1/4 ounces) white *or* yellow cake mix**
 1-1/2   **cups whipped topping**
     1   **can (8 ounces) crushed pineapple, well drained**
   1/4   **cup flaked coconut, toasted**

In a small bowl, whisk the milk and pudding mix for 2 minutes. Let stand for 2 minutes or until soft-set; cover and refrigerate.

Grease the bottom of two 8-in. square baking dishes. Prepare cake batter according to package directions; pour into prepared dishes. Bake at 350° for 20-25 minutes or until a toothpick inserted near the center comes out clean. Cool for 5 minutes before removing from pans to wire racks to cool completely.

Fold whipped topping into pudding until blended. Level cake tops if necessary. Place one cake on a serving plate; spread with half of the pudding mixture. Top with pineapple, and the remaining cake and pudding mixture. Sprinkle with coconut. Store in the refrigerator. **yield: 12-16 servings.**

yum-yum cake

chocolate layer cake

chocolate layer cake

Taste of Home Test Kitchen • Greendale, Wisconsin
Our home economists created this eye-catching dessert. No one will suspect this layered chocolate cake, brimming with sweet citrus flavor, is light!

      1   **package (18-1/4 ounces) chocolate cake mix**
1-1/4   **cups buttermilk**
      1   **egg**
      4   **egg whites**
ORANGE FILLING:
      1   **cup cold fat-free milk**
      1   **package (3.3 ounces) instant white chocolate pudding mix** *or* **1 package (3.4 ounces) instant vanilla pudding mix**
   1/4   **teaspoon grated orange peel**
   1/8   **teaspoon orange extract**
   1/2   **cup heavy whipping cream, whipped**
CHOCOLATE GLAZE:
      3   **squares (1 ounce** *each***) semisweet chocolate, chopped**
      1   **tablespoon fat-free milk**
1-1/2   **teaspoons butter**

Coat three 9-in. round baking pans with cooking spray and line with waxed paper. Coat waxed paper with cooking spray and dust with flour; set aside.

In a large bowl, beat the first four ingredients on low speed for 30 seconds. Beat on medium for 2 minutes. Pour into prepared pans.

Bake at 350° for 20-25 minutes or until a toothpick inserted near the center comes out clean. Cool for 10 minutes before removing to wire racks to cool. Gently peel off waxed paper.

In a large bowl, whisk first four filling ingredients for 2 minutes. Let stand for 2 minutes or until soft-set. Fold in whipped cream.

Place one cake layer on a serving plate; top with half of the filling. Repeat layers. Top with the third cake layer. In a microwave-safe bowl, microwave the glaze ingredients, uncovered, at 30% power for 45 seconds; stir until smooth. Spread over top of cake. **yield: 12 servings.**

citrus sherbet torte

Betty Tabb • Mifflintown, Pennsylvania
When my mother-in-law first served this torte, I thought it was the most attractive dessert I ever saw. It keeps well in the freezer, and different flavors of sherbet can be used to reflect the colors of the season.

      1   **package (16 ounces) angel food cake mix**
      2   **pints orange sherbet**
      2   **pints lime sherbet**
      1   **carton (12 ounces) frozen whipped topping, thawed**
Assorted cake decorator sprinkles, optional

Prepare and bake cake according to package directions, using an ungreased 10-in. tube pan. Cool.

Immediately invert pan; cool completely, about 1 hour. Run a knife around side and center tube of pan; split horizontally into three layers.

Place bottom layer on a serving plate; spread with orange sherbet. Top with the second layer; spread with lime sherbet. Top with remaining cake layer. Frost top and sides of cake with whipped topping. Decorate with colored sprinkles if desired. Freeze until serving. **yield: 12-14 servings.**

citrus sherbet torte

Doris Grotz
York, Nebraska
This rich torte is so impressive, thanks to its combination of moist cake layers, chocolate-almond and cream fillings, cherry topping and almond-studded sides. It's almost too pretty to cut! Don't hesitate, though—no one will be able to resist a slice, no matter how stuffed they are.

black forest torte

2/3	**cup butter, softened**
1-3/4	**cups sugar**
4	**eggs**
1-1/4	**cups water**
4	**squares (1 ounce *each*) unsweetened chocolate**
1	**teaspoon vanilla extract**
1-3/4	**cups all-purpose flour**
1	**teaspoon baking powder**
1/4	**teaspoon baking soda**

CHOCOLATE FILLING:

6	**ounces German sweet chocolate**
3/4	**cup butter, cubed**
1/2	**cup sliced almonds, toasted**

CREAM FILLING:

3	**cups heavy whipping cream**
2	**tablespoons sugar**
2	**teaspoons vanilla extract**

TOPPING:

1	**cup cherry pie filling**
3	**cups sliced almonds, toasted**

In a large bowl, cream butter and sugar until light and fluffy. Add the eggs, one at a time, beating well after each addition. Beat in water just until blended.

In a microwave, melt chocolate; stir until smooth. Stir in vanilla until blended. Combine the flour, baking powder and baking soda; add to creamed mixture alternately with chocolate mixture, beating well after each addition.

Pour into four greased and floured 9-in. round baking pans. Bake at 350° for 15-20 minutes or until a toothpick inserted near the center comes out clean. Cool for 10 minutes before removing from pans to wire racks to cool completely.

For chocolate filling, in a microwave, melt chocolate; stir until smooth. Stir in butter until smooth. Add almonds.

For cream filling, in a small bowl, beat cream until it begins to thicken. Add sugar and vanilla; beat until soft peaks form.

To assemble, place one cake on a serving platter; spread with a fourth of the chocolate filling and a fourth of the cream filling. Repeat layers twice. Top with remaining cake and chocolate filling.

Place 1-1/2 cups of the remaining cream filling in a pastry bag with a large star pastry tip. Pipe around edge of cake. Fill center with cherry pie filling. Spread remaining cream filling over sides of cake; press almonds into sides. Store in the refrigerator. **yield: 16 servings.**

chocolate lover's delight

chocolate hazelnut torte, p. 48

Chocolate lovers *everywhere will appreciate this chapter's assortment of yummy, tempting and the most indulgent of treats. Here, you'll find a tantalizing collection of cakes, tortes, cookies, brownies, fudge and bite-sized confections, all proud to be members of the chocolate family. These blissful treasures are sure to bring big smiles and keep guests asking for more.*

dark chocolate layer cake

minutes before removing from pans to wire racks to cool completely. For frosting, combine the cream, sugar and corn syrup in a small saucepan. Bring to a full boil over medium heat, stirring constantly. Remove from the heat; stir in chocolate and butter until melted.

Transfer to a large bowl. Cover and refrigerate until desired consistency, stirring occasionally. Spread frosting between layers and over top and sides of cake. Store in the refrigerator. **yield: 12 servings.**

chocolate cream bonbons

Joan Lewis • Reno, Nevada
My grandmother gave me this tasty recipe when I was a girl. Some of my fondest childhood memories are of her huge kitchen and all the delicious treats she made.

4	cups confectioners' sugar
1	cup ground pecans *or* walnuts
1/2	cup plus 2 tablespoons sweetened condensed milk
1/4	cup butter, softened
3	cups (18 ounces) semisweet chocolate chips
2	tablespoons shortening

In a large bowl, combine the confectioners' sugar, ground pecans, milk and butter. Roll into 1-in. balls. Place on waxed paper-lined baking sheets. Cover and refrigerate overnight.

In a microwave, melt chocolate chips and shortening; stir until smooth. Dip balls in chocolate; allow excess to drip off. Place on waxed paper; let stand until set. (If balls are too soft to dip, place in the freezer for a few minutes first.) **yield: about 6 dozen.**

dark chocolate layer cake

David Heppner • Brandon, Florida
A slice of this classic cake is sure to satisfy any chocolate craving. It's rich, delectable and simply irresistible.

3	cups sugar
1-1/2	cups buttermilk
1-1/2	cups brewed coffee, cooled
3	eggs
3/4	cup canola oil
3	squares (1 ounces *each*) semisweet chocolate, melted
3/4	teaspoon vanilla extract
2-1/2	cups all-purpose flour
1-1/2	cups baking cocoa
2	teaspoons baking soda
3/4	teaspoon baking powder
1-1/4	teaspoons salt

FROSTING:

1	cup heavy whipping cream
2	tablespoons sugar
2	tablespoons light corn syrup
16	squares (1 ounce *each*) semisweet chocolate
1/4	cup butter

In a large bowl, beat the sugar, buttermilk, coffee, eggs, oil, chocolate and vanilla until well blended. In another large bowl, combine the flour, cocoa, baking soda, baking powder and salt; gradually beat into buttermilk mixture until blended.

Pour into three greased and floured 9-in. round baking pans. Bake at 350° for 30-35 minutes or until a toothpick inserted near the center comes out clean. Cool for 10

chocolate cream bonbons

chocolate-covered white cheesecake

DESSERT *Tip*

You want a flat top when decorating a cheesecake with a glaze. One reason a cake crowns, or ends up with a rounded top, is that the oven temperature is too high. To avoid this, use a thermometer to check the temperature of your oven.

Carol Staniger
Springdale, Arkansas
The inside scoop on this tasty treat is the white chocolate center. Drizzling melted vanilla chips on top of the chocolate glaze makes for a pretty presentation.

chocolate-covered white cheesecake

1-1/2 cups chocolate wafer crumbs (about 27 wafers)
3 tablespoons butter, melted

FILLING:
3 packages (8 ounces *each*) cream cheese, softened
1/2 cup sugar
1/4 cup heavy whipping cream
1 teaspoon vanilla extract
3 eggs, lightly beaten
1-1/2 cups vanilla *or* white chips, melted and cooled

GLAZE:
2 cups (12 ounces) semisweet chocolate chips
1 cup heavy whipping cream
2 tablespoons butter
2 tablespoons sugar
1 cup vanilla *or* white chips, melted and cooled
Striped chocolate kisses, optional
Raspberries, optional

In a small bowl, combine wafer crumbs and butter; press into the bottom of a greased 9-in. springform pan. Place pan on a baking sheet. Bake at 350° for 10 minutes. Cool on a wire rack.

In a large bowl, beat the cream cheese, sugar, cream and vanilla until smooth. Add eggs; beat on low speed just until combined. Stir in melted vanilla chips. Pour into crust. Place pan on a double thickness of heavy-duty foil (about 16 in. x 16 in.). Securely wrap foil around pan.

Place springform pan in a larger baking pan. Add 1 in. hot water to larger pan. Bake at 350° for 65-70 minutes or until center is almost set. Remove pan from water bath. Cool on a wire rack for 10 minutes. Carefully run a knife around edge of pan to loosen; cool 1 hour longer. Refrigerate overnight.

For the glaze, place chocolate chips in a large bowl; set aside. In a heavy saucepan, bring the cream, butter and sugar to a boil over medium-high heat, stirring constantly. Pour over chocolate chips. Cool for 3 minutes. Stir until smooth and cool.

Remove the sides of pan. Spread glaze over the top and sides of cheesecake. Refrigerate for 2 hours.

Drizzle melted vanilla chips over cheesecake. Garnish with kisses and raspberries if desired. Refrigerate leftovers. **yield: 12-14 servings.**

mud pie

Sandra Ashcraft • Pueblo, Colorado
We enjoyed this cool, delicious pie while on a trip to California more than 20 years ago. After we returned, I hit the kitchen and developed my own recipe. The results were fantastic!

1-1/2   cups chocolate wafer crumbs
1/3   cup butter, melted
1   quart chocolate ice cream, softened
1   quart coffee ice cream, softened
CHOCOLATE SAUCE:
2   tablespoons butter
2   squares (1 ounce *each*) unsweetened chocolate
1   cup sugar
1/4   teaspoon salt
1   can (5 ounces) evaporated milk
1/2   teaspoon vanilla extract
WHIPPED CREAM:
1   cup heavy whipping cream
1   tablespoon sugar

In a small bowl, combine wafer crumbs and butter. Press onto the bottom and up the sides of an ungreased 9-in. deep-dish pie plate. Bake at 350° for 10 minutes. Cool on a wire rack.

In a large bowl, beat chocolate ice cream and coffee ice cream. Spoon into crust. Cover and freeze for 8 hours or overnight.

mud pie

For chocolate sauce, in a small saucepan, melt butter and chocolate over low heat; stir until smooth. Stir in the sugar, salt and evaporated milk. Bring to a boil, stirring constantly. Remove from the heat; stir in vanilla. Set aside.

Remove pie from the freezer 15 minutes before serving. In a small bowl, beat cream until it begins to thicken. Gradually add sugar; beat until soft peaks form.

Drizzle three stripes of chocolate sauce into a pastry bag; carefully add whipped cream. Pipe onto each slice of pie. Serve with remaining chocolate sauce. **yield: 8 servings.**

chocolate clusters

Sara Ann Fowler • Illinois City, Illinois
No-bake cookies are so easy to do. These delightful treats are a cross between a cookie and candy.

2   pounds white chocolate *or* almond bark
1   cup creamy *or* chunky peanut butter
2   cups salted dry roasted peanuts
3   cups pastel miniature marshmallows
4   cups crisp rice cereal

Melt white chocolate and peanut butter in microwave or double boiler, stirring often to mix well. Add all remaining ingredients; stir with wooden spoon to coat evenly. Drop by teaspoonfuls onto waxed paper. **yield: 11 dozen.**

triple chocolate delight

Mrs. Edwin Hill • Santa Barbara, California
A fitting finale for any special occasion, this fudgy cake has three luscious layers chocolate lovers can sink their teeth into.

1   cup butter, softened, *divided*
2   cups sugar
4   eggs
5   Milky Way candy bars (2.15 ounces *each*)
1-1/4   cups buttermilk
2-1/2   cups all-purpose flour
1/2   teaspoon baking soda
1/4   teaspoon salt
1   cup chopped walnuts
FROSTING:
1/2   cup butter, *divided*
2-1/2   cups sugar
1   cup evaporated milk

1 jar (7 ounces) marshmallow creme
1 cup (6 ounces) semisweet chocolate chips
Chopped walnuts, optional

In a large bowl, cream 1/2 cup butter and sugar until light and fluffy. Add eggs, one at a time, beating well after each addition.

In a heavy saucepan, stir candy bars and remaining butter over low heat until melted. Remove from the heat; stir in buttermilk.

Combine the flour, baking soda and salt; add alternately with buttermilk mixture to creamed mixture, beating well after each addition. Fold in nuts.

Pour into three greased and floured 9-in. round baking pans. Bake at 350° for 30-40 minutes or until a toothpick inserted near the center comes out clean. Cool for 10 minutes before removing from pans to wire racks to cool completely.

For frosting, lightly grease the sides of a large saucepan with 1 tablespoon of butter; set remaining butter aside. Combine sugar and milk; cook over medium heat, stirring occasionally, until mixture comes to a rolling boil. Boil until a candy thermometer reads 234° (soft-ball stage). Remove from the heat; stir in marshmallow creme, chips and remaining butter.

Transfer to a large bowl; cool to 110°. Beat on medium speed until smooth, about 5-7 minutes. Spread frosting between layers and over the top and sides of cake. Sprinkle with walnuts if desired. **yield: 12 servings.**

triple chocolate delight

chocolate covered cherries

chocolate covered cherries

Linda Hammerich • Bonanza, Oregon
These chocolate-covered cherry confections are a wonderful addition to any dessert platter. They're easy to make and disappear fast!

2-1/2 cups confectioners' sugar
1/4 cup butter, softened
1 tablespoon milk
1/2 teaspoon almond extract
2 jars (8 ounces *each*) maraschino cherries with stems, well drained
2 cups (12 ounces) semisweet chocolate chips
2 tablespoons shortening

In a small bowl, combine the sugar, butter, milk and extract. Knead until smooth and pliable. Shape into 1-in. balls and flatten each into a 2-in. circle.

Wrap one circle around each cherry and lightly roll in hands. Place with stems up on waxed paper-lined baking sheet. Cover loosely and refrigerate for 4 hours or overnight.

In a microwave, melt chocolate and shortening; stir until smooth. Holding onto the stems, dip cherries into chocolate; allow excess to drip off. Place on waxed paper until set. Store in a covered container. Refrigerate 1-2 weeks before serving. **yield: 3 dozen.**

Gently spoon into an ungreased 10-in. tube pan. Cut through batter with a knife to remove air pockets. Bake on the lowest oven rack at 325° for 60-65 minutes or until cake springs back when lightly touched. Immediately invert pan; cool completely, about 1 hour.

Run a knife around side and center tube of pan. Remove cake to a serving plate. For filling, in a large bowl, combine all ingredients until smooth; refrigerate for 1 hour.

Beat until stiff peaks form. Cut a 1-in. slice off the top of the cake; set aside. To make a tunnel, carefully hollow out bottom, leaving a 1-in. shell. Fill tunnel with some of the filling; replace cake top. Spread remaining filling over top and sides of cake. Store in the refrigerator. **yield: 12 servings.**

chocolate lover's chiffon cake

Joann Plate • Oskaloosa, Iowa
This cake is always requested at our house. It is guaranteed to satisfy any craving for chocolate!

1	cup egg whites (about 7)
1/2	cup baking cocoa
3/4	cup boiling water
1-3/4	cups cake flour
1-3/4	cups sugar
1-1/2	teaspoons baking soda
1	teaspoon salt
1/2	cup canola oil
7	egg yolks
2	teaspoons vanilla extract
1/2	teaspoon cream of tartar

FILLING:

3	cups heavy whipping cream
1-1/2	cups confectioners' sugar
3/4	cup baking cocoa
2	teaspoons vanilla extract
1/4	teaspoon salt

Place egg whites in a large bowl; set aside for 30 minutes. Meanwhile, stir cocoa and water in a small bowl until smooth. Cool.

In a large bowl, combine the flour, sugar, baking soda and salt. In another bowl, whisk the oil, egg yolks, vanilla and cocoa mixture. Add to dry ingredients; beat until well blended. In another bowl, beat egg whites and cream of tartar until stiff peaks form; fold into batter.

fudge truffle cheesecake

S.E. Sanborn • Perry, Michigan
This cheesecake is perfect for a holiday gathering. It serves a lot of people, and everyone savors the chocolaty flavor.

CRUST:

1-1/2	cups vanilla wafer crumbs (about 45 wafers)
1/2	cup confectioners' sugar
1/3	cup baking cocoa
1/3	cup butter, melted

FILLING:

3	packages (8 ounces *each*) cream cheese, softened
1	can (14 ounces) sweetened condensed milk
2	teaspoons vanilla extract
4	eggs, lightly beaten
2	cups (12 ounces) semisweet chocolate chips, melted and cooled

Whipped cream and additional chocolate chips, optional

Combine all crust ingredients and press onto the bottom and 2 in. up the sides of a 9-in. springform pan; chill.

For filling, beat the cream cheese, milk and vanilla in a large bowl until smooth. Add eggs; beat on low speed just until combined. Stir in melted chips. Pour into crust. Place pan on a baking sheet.

Bake at 350° for 60-65 minutes or until center is almost set. Cool on a wire rack for 10 minutes. Carefully run a knife around edge of pan to loosen; cool 1 hour longer. Refrigerate overnight.

Garnish with whipped cream and chocolate chips if desired. **yield: 12-16 servings.**

three-layer chocolate brownies

three-layer chocolate brownies

Billie Hopkins • Enterprise, Oregon
I often serve these hearty, cake-like brownies with a fork for easier eating. The oatmeal crust, fudgy filling and chocolate frosting make them a hit wherever I take them.

1	cup quick-cooking oats
1/2	cup packed brown sugar
1/3	cup all-purpose flour
1/4	teaspoon baking soda
1/4	teaspoon salt
1/4	cup butter, melted

FILLING:

1/2	cup butter
2	squares (1 ounce *each*) semisweet chocolate
1	cup sugar
2	eggs, lightly beaten
1/4	cup milk
2	teaspoons vanilla extract
2/3	cup all-purpose flour
1/4	teaspoon baking soda
1/4	teaspoon salt

FROSTING:

3	tablespoons butter, softened
1	square (1 ounce) unsweetened chocolate, melted
1	cup confectioners' sugar
1	tablespoon milk
3/4	teaspoon vanilla extract

In a small bowl, combine the first six ingredients; beat on low speed until blended. Press into a greased 9-in. square baking pan. Bake at 350° for 10 minutes.

Meanwhile, in a large saucepan over low heat, melt butter and chocolate. Remove from the heat; stir in the sugar, eggs, milk and vanilla. Combine the flour, baking soda and salt; gradually stir into the chocolate mixture until smooth. Pour over crust.

Bake for 35-40 minutes or until the top springs back when lightly touched. Cool on wire rack.

In a small bowl, combine the frosting ingredients; beat until smooth. Frost cooled brownies. **yield: 1-1/2 dozen.**

double chocolate cookies

Chantal Cornwall • Prince Rupert, British Columbia
When I make these yummy treats with my grandson, Ben, I use an extra-large mixing bowl to prevent the flour and other ingredients from spattering to every corner of my kitchen. He enjoys making the cookies almost as much as eating them!

1-1/4	cups butter, softened
2	cups sugar
2	eggs
2	teaspoons vanilla extract
2	cups all-purpose flour
3/4	cup baking cocoa
1	teaspoon baking soda
1/2	teaspoon salt
2	cups (12 ounces) semisweet chocolate chips

In a large bowl, cream butter and sugar until light and fluffy. Beat in eggs and vanilla. Combine the flour, cocoa, baking soda and salt; gradually add to creamed mixture and mix well. Stir in chocolate chips.

Drop by rounded teaspoonfuls 2 in. apart onto greased baking sheets. Bake at 350° for 8-10 minutes or until set. Cool for 2 minutes before removing from pans to wire racks. **yield: about 9 dozen.**

double chocolate cookies

The next time you're whipping up a recipe that calls for dusting the pan with flour—and the batter is chocolate—simply "flour" with baking cocoa instead. The cocoa will enhance the chocolate flavor and eliminate any white flour dust scattered over the baked goods.

Taste of Home Test Kitchen Greendale, Wisconsin
Guests will be surprised to learn this dessert from our Test Kitchen starts with a convenient cake mix. Each bite features chocolate, almonds and apricots.

chocolate-almond sacher torte

chocolate-almond sacher torte

1/2	cup chopped dried apricots
1/2	cup amaretto
1	package (18-1/4 ounces) devil's food cake mix
3/4	cup water
1/3	cup canola oil
3	eggs

APRICOT FILLING:

2/3	cup apricot preserves
1	tablespoon amaretto

FROSTING:

1/2	cup butter, softened
4-1/2	cups confectioners' sugar
3/4	cup baking cocoa
1/3	cup boiling water
1	tablespoon amaretto
1	cup sliced almonds, toasted

In a small bowl, combine apricots and amaretto; let stand for 15 minutes. In a large bowl, combine the cake mix, water, oil, eggs and apricots. Beat on low speed for 30 seconds; beat on medium for 2 minutes.

Pour into two greased and floured 9-in. round baking pans. Bake at 350° for 25-30 minutes or until a toothpick inserted near the center comes out clean. Cool for 10 minutes before removing from pans to wire racks to cool completely.

For filling, in a small saucepan, heat apricot preserves and amaretto on low until preserves are melted, stirring occasionally; set aside.

For frosting, in a large bowl, cream the butter, confectioners' sugar and cocoa until light and fluffy. Add water and amaretto. Beat on low until combined. Beat on medium for 1 minute or until frosting achieves spreading consistency.

Cut each cake horizontally into two layers. Place a bottom layer on a serving plate; spread with half of the filling. Top with another cake layer; spread with 2/3 cup frosting. Top with third layer and remaining filling. Top with remaining cake layer.

Frost top and sides of cake with remaining frosting. Gently press almonds into the sides. Cover and refrigerate for several hours before slicing. **yield: 12-16 servings.**

mocha chip cheesecake

Renee Gastineau • Seattle, Washington

Two favorite flavors—coffee and chocolate—combine in this blissful treat. The chocolate crumb crust and sprinkling of chocolate chips contrast wonderfully with the creamy coffee filling. When you're offering slices of this cheesecake, few people can resist!

CRUST:
- 2 cups chocolate wafer crumbs (about 32 wafers)
- 1/2 cup sugar
- 1/2 cup butter, melted

FILLING:
- 3 packages (8 ounces *each*) cream cheese, softened
- 1 cup sugar
- 3 tablespoons all-purpose flour
- 4 eggs, lightly beaten
- 1/3 cup heavy whipping cream
- 1 tablespoon instant coffee granules
- 1 teaspoon vanilla extract
- 1 cup (6 ounces) miniature semisweet chocolate chips, *divided*

In a large bowl, combine crumbs and sugar; stir in butter. Press onto the bottom and 2 in. up the sides of a greased 9-in. springform pan; set aside.

In a large bowl, beat cream cheese and sugar until smooth. Add flour and beat well. Add eggs, beating on low speed just until combined.

mocha chip cheesecake

chocolate mousse

In a small bowl, combine cream and coffee; let stand for 1 minute. Add to cream cheese mixture with vanilla; beat just until combined. Stir in 3/4 cup chocolate chips. Pour into crust. Sprinkle with remaining chocolate chips.

Bake at 325° for 50-55 minutes or until center is almost set. Cool on a wire rack for 1 hour. Refrigerate overnight.

Let stand at room temperature for 30 minutes before slicing. **yield: 12-14 servings.**

chocolate mousse

Judy Spencer • San Diego, California

I love to cook and have tons of recipes, but this one is a favorite and always draws raves. Best of all, it's easy to make.

- 1/4 cup semisweet chocolate chips
- 1 tablespoon water
- 1 egg yolk, lightly beaten
- 1-1/2 teaspoons vanilla extract
- 1/2 cup whipping cream
- 1 tablespoon sugar

Whipped cream, optional

In a small saucepan, melt chocolate chips with water; stir until smooth. Stir a small amount of hot chocolate mixture into egg yolk; return all to the pan, stirring constantly. Cook and stir for 2 minutes or until slightly thickened. Remove from the heat; stir in vanilla. Cool, stirring several times.

In a small bowl, beat whipping cream until it begins to thicken. Add sugar; beat until soft peaks form. Fold in cooled chocolate mixture. Cover and refrigerate for at least 2 hours. Garnish with whipped cream if desired. **yield: 2 servings.**

chocolate cinnamon mud balls

thermometer reads 238° (soft-ball stage). Remove from the heat. Cool, without stirring, until mixture reaches 110°.

Transfer to a large bowl; add the cinnamon, vanilla and salt. Beat until light-colored and stiff enough to knead, about 2 minutes. Knead mixture in bowl for 2 minutes or until smooth. Roll into 1-in. balls; cover and freeze for 20 minutes.

In a microwave, melt chips and shortening; stir until smooth. Dip balls in chocolate; allow excess to drip off. Roll in nuts if desired. Place on waxed paper; let stand until set. **yield: 3 dozen.**

editor's note: We recommend that you test your candy thermometer before each use by bringing water to a boil; the thermometer should read 212°. Adjust your recipe temperature up or down based on your test.

chocolate hazelnut torte

Taste of Home Test Kitchen • Greendale, Wisconsin
Most cake recipes feed a group. So our home economists came up with this six-serving cake. That's enough for two…with just the right amount of leftovers!

1/3	cup butter, softened
1	cup packed brown sugar
1	egg
1	teaspoon vanilla extract
1	cup all-purpose flour
1/4	cup baking cocoa
1	teaspoon baking soda
1/8	teaspoon salt
1/2	cup sour cream
1/2	cup brewed coffee, room temperature

chocolate cinnamon mud balls

Marlene Gates • Bozeman, Montana
A friend's mother who knows I love to cook shared this recipe. These delicious candies won a blue ribbon at our local fair!

2	cups sugar
1/2	cup water
1/4	cup heavy whipping cream
1	tablespoon light corn syrup
1-1/2	squares (1-1/2 ounces) semisweet baking chocolate, chopped
1	to 2 teaspoons ground cinnamon
1	teaspoon vanilla extract
Pinch salt	
2-1/2	cups (15 ounces) semisweet chocolate chips
1	tablespoon shortening
1/2	cup ground nuts, optional

Butter the sides of a heavy saucepan; add the first five ingredients. Cook and stir over medium-high heat until sugar is dissolved. Cook, without stirring, until a candy

chocolate hazelnut torte

FROSTING:
- 7 squares (1 ounce *each*) semisweet chocolate, chopped
- 1 cup heavy whipping cream
- 2 tablespoons sugar
- 1/3 cup chocolate hazelnut spread

Chocolate curls and hazelnuts, optional

In a small bowl, cream butter and brown sugar until light and fluffy. Beat in egg and vanilla. Combine the flour, cocoa, baking soda and salt; gradually add to creamed mixture alternately with sour cream and coffee. Beat just until combined.

Pour into two greased and floured 6-in. round baking pans. Bake at 350° for 25-30 minutes or until a knife inserted near the center comes out clean. Cool for 10 minutes before removing from pans to wire racks to cool completely.

For frosting, in a small saucepan, melt chocolate with cream and sugar over low heat; stir until smooth. Remove from the heat; whisk in hazelnut spread. Transfer to a small bowl; cover and refrigerate until frosting reaches spreading consistency, stirring occasionally.

Spread frosting between layers and over the top and sides of cake. Garnish with chocolate curls and hazelnuts if desired. **yield: 6 servings.**

chocolate ice cream

Kathryn Herman • Villisca, Iowa

This is, without a doubt, the best ice cream I've ever had. Our family loves to make homemade ice cream when we get together for birthday dinners, and this is our favorite flavor.

- 4 cups milk
- 1 eggs, lightly beaten
- 2 egg yolks, lightly beaten
- 2 cups sugar
- 1/3 cup baking cocoa
- 2 tablespoons all-purpose flour
- 2 cans (12 ounces *each*) evaporated milk
- 2 tablespoons vanilla extract

Milk

In a heavy saucepan, combine the first six ingredients. Cook until thickened. Add evaporated milk; bring to a boil. Remove from heat and cool. Add vanilla.

Pour into the cylinder of an ice cream freezer; add enough milk to fill cylinder three-fourths full. Freeze according to manufacturer's directions. When ice cream is frozen, transfer to a freezer container; freeze for 2-4 hours before serving. **yield: about 2-1/2 quarts.**

mamie eisenhower's fudge

mamie eisenhower's fudge

Linda First • Hinsdale, Illinois

My mother came across this recipe in a newspaper some 40 years ago. One taste and you'll see why it doesn't take long for a big batch to disappear.

- 1 tablespoon plus 1/2 cup butter, *divided*
- 3 milk chocolate candy bars (two 7 ounces, one 1.55 ounces), broken into pieces
- 4 cups (24 ounces) semisweet chocolate chips
- 1 jar (7 ounces) marshmallow creme
- 1 can (12 ounces) evaporated milk
- 4-1/2 cups sugar
- 2 cups chopped walnuts

Line a 13-in. x 9-in. pan with foil and butter the foil with 1 tablespoon butter; set aside. In a large heat-proof bowl, combine the candy bars, chocolate chips and marshmallow creme; set aside.

In a large heavy saucepan over medium-low heat, combine the milk, sugar and remaining butter. Bring to a boil, stirring constantly. Boil and stir for 4-1/2 minutes. Pour over chocolate mixture; stir until chocolate is melted and mixture is smooth and creamy. Stir in walnuts. Pour into prepared pan. Cover and refrigerate until firm.

Using foil, lift fudge out of pan; cut into 1-in. squares. Store in an airtight container in the refrigerator. **yield: about 6 pounds.**

victorian strawberry chocolate cake

Amy Parker • Ponca City, Oklahoma
With its alternating light and dark layers, thick chocolate frosting and fresh strawberry garnishes, this heart-shaped cake will be a hit for any occasion.

2	cups boiling water
1	cup baking cocoa
1	cup butter, softened
2-1/2	cups sugar
4	eggs
1-1/2	teaspoons vanilla extract
2-3/4	cups all-purpose flour
2	teaspoons baking powder
2	teaspoons baking soda
1	quart fresh strawberries
1	cup (6 ounces) semisweet chocolate chips, melted

FROSTING:

2/3	cup shortening
1	package (32 ounces) confectioners' sugar
1/2	cup water

ICING:

1-1/2	cups semisweet chocolate chips
1/3	cup heavy whipping cream

Chocolate shavings and additional confectioners' sugar, optional

In a small bowl, combine water and cocoa until blended; set aside. In a large bowl, cream butter, sugar until light and fluffy. Add eggs, one at a time, beating well after each addition. Beat in vanilla. Combine the flour, baking powder and baking soda; add to the creamed mixture alternately with cocoa mixture, beating well after each addition.

Pour into two greased and floured 9-in. heart-shaped pans. Bake at 350° for 35-40 minutes or until a toothpick inserted near the center comes out clean. Cool for 10 minutes before removing from pans to wire racks to cool completely.

Slice 10 strawberries; set aside. Dip remaining whole strawberries into melted chocolate, about three-fourths to top; allowing excess to drip off. Place on a waxed paper-lined baking sheet; refrigerate until set.

For frosting, cream shortening and confectioners' sugar in a large bowl until light and fluffy; gradually add water, beating until smooth. Spread between layers and over top and sides of the cake. Set aside to set, about 30 minutes.

For icing, heat chocolate chips and cream in a small saucepan over medium heat until chocolate is melted, stirring occasionally. Spread over frosted cake until smooth. Refrigerate until set.

Before serving, arrange two rows of sliced strawberries on top of cake in a heart shape. Fill the center with chocolate shavings and dust with confectioners' sugar if desired. Place dipped strawberries around base. Store in the refrigerator. **yield: 10-12 servings.**

candy bar fudge

Mary Lou Bridge • Taylor Ridge, Illinois
I created this recipe to duplicate a delightful, rich fudge I tried in a candy shop. It's simple to make and will melt in your mouth.

6	Snickers candy bars (2.07 ounces *each*)
3	cups sugar
3/4	cup butter
2/3	cup evaporated milk
2	cups (12 ounces) semisweet chocolate chips
1	jar (7 ounces) marshmallow creme
1	teaspoon vanilla extract

Line a 9-in. square pan with foil. Butter the foil and set pan aside. Cut candy bars into 1/2-in. slices; set aside.

In a heavy saucepan, bring sugar, butter and milk to a boil over medium heat. Cook and stir until a candy thermometer reads 234° (soft-ball stage), about 3 minutes. Remove from the heat. Stir in chocolate chips, marshmallow creme and vanilla until smooth.

Pour half into prepared pan. Sprinkle with candy bar slices. Top with remaining chocolate mixture and spread

victorian strawberry chocolate cake

evenly. Let stand at room temperature to cool. Lift out of pan and remove foil. Cut into squares. **yield: 4 pounds (about 7 dozen).**

editor's note: We recommend that you test your candy thermometer before each use by bringing water to a boil; the thermometer should read 212°. Adjust your recipe temperature up or down based on your test.

fudgy brownies

Evie Gloistein • Susanville, California
I can stir up these moist and chocolaty brownies in a snap. They're oh-so-easy to make and oh-so-scrumptious to eat.

1/2	cup butter
4	squares (1 ounce *each*) unsweetened chocolate
2	cups sugar
4	eggs, lightly beaten
1	teaspoon vanilla extract
1/2	cup all-purpose flour
1/2	teaspoon salt
2	cups chopped pecans, optional

Confectioners' sugar, optional

In a microwave, melt butter and chocolate; stir until smooth. Cool slightly. In a large bowl, beat sugar and eggs. Stir in vanilla and chocolate mixture. Combine flour and salt; gradually add to chocolate mixture. Stir in pecans if desired.

Spread into two greased 8-in. square baking pans. Bake at 325° for 35-40 minutes or until a toothpick inserted near the center comes out clean. Cool on a wire rack. Dust with confectioners' sugar if desired. Cut into bars. **yield: 32 brownies.**

fudgy brownies

chocolate trifle

chocolate trifle

Pam Botine • Goldsboro, North Carolina
For a fabulous finale when entertaining, this lovely layered trifle is a winner! It's a make-ahead dessert that serves a group, and it even tastes great the next day.

1	package (18-1/4 ounces) chocolate fudge cake mix
1	package (6 ounces) instant chocolate pudding mix
1/2	cup strong coffee
1	carton (12 ounces) frozen whipped topping, thawed
6	Heath bars (1.4 ounces *each*), crushed

Bake cake according to the package directions. Cool. Prepare pudding according to the package directions; set aside.

Crumble cake; reserve 1/2 cup. Place half of the remaining cake crumbs in the bottom of a 4-1/2- or 5-qt. trifle dish or decorative glass bowl.

Layer with half of the coffee, half of the pudding, half of the whipped topping and half of the crushed candy bars. Repeat the layers of cake, coffee, pudding and whipped topping.

Combine remaining crushed candy bars with reserved cake crumbs; sprinkle over top. Refrigerate 4-5 hours before serving. **yield: 8-10 servings.**

cakes galore

raspberry butter torte, p. 62

Cake is the royalty of all desserts. Whether it's a light and airy angel food cake, a moist, cream-filled roll or an impressive three-layer crowned with frosting, each unforgettable bite always hits the sweet spot. There's simply no better way to celebrate any occasion, big or small, than with cake. So turn the page to find an array of splendid choices, from simple to lavish, to make the moment memorable.

italian cream cheese cake

In a large bowl, beat cream cheese and butter until smooth. Beat in confectioners' sugar and vanilla until fluffy. Stir in pecans. Spread frosting between layers and over top and sides of cake. Store in the refrigerator. **yield: 12 servings.**

lemon poppy seed cake

Betty Bjarnason • Egbert, Ontario
I complete this delightful cake by brushing on sweetened lemon juice and dusting it with confectioners' sugar.

  1   **package (18-1/4 ounces) lemon cake mix**
  1   **package (3.4 ounces) instant lemon pudding mix**
3/4 **cup warm water**
1/2 **cup canola oil**
  4   **eggs**
  1   **teaspoon lemon extract**
  1   **teaspoon almond extract**
1/3 **cup poppy seeds**
1/2 **cup confectioners' sugar**
Juice of 1 lemon
Additional confectioners' sugar, optional

In a large bowl, combine cake and pudding mixes. Add the water, oil, eggs and extracts. Beat for 30 seconds on low speed. Beat for 2 minutes on medium speed. Stir in the poppy seeds. Pour into a greased 12-cup fluted tube pan.

Bake at 350° for 50-60 minutes or until a toothpick inserted near the center comes out clean. Cool in pan 10 minutes before inverting onto a serving plate.

Combine confectioners' sugar and lemon juice; brush over the warm cake. Cool. Dust with the additional confectioners' sugar if desired. **yield: 12-16 servings.**

italian cream cheese cake

Joyce Lutz • Centerview, Missouri
I bake this Italian cream cheese cake year-round. Buttermilk makes every bite of this luscious dessert moist and flavorful.

1/2   **cup butter, softened**
1/2   **cup shortening**
  2   **cups sugar**
  5   **eggs,** *separated*
  1   **teaspoon vanilla extract**
  2   **cups all-purpose flour**
  1   **teaspoon baking soda**
  1   **cup buttermilk**
1-1/2 **cups flaked coconut**
  1   **cup chopped pecans**
CREAM CHEESE FROSTING:
  2   **packages (one 8 ounces, one 3 ounces) cream cheese, softened**
3/4   **cup butter, softened**
  6   **cups confectioners' sugar**
1-1/2 **teaspoons vanilla extract**
3/4   **cup chopped pecans**

In a large bowl, cream the butter, shortening and sugar until light and fluffy. Beat in the egg yolks and vanilla. Combine the flour and baking soda; add to creamed mixture alternately with buttermilk. Beat just until combined. Stir in the coconut and pecans.

In a small bowl, beat egg whites until stiff peaks form. Fold a fourth of the egg whites into batter, then fold in remaining whites. Pour into three greased and floured 9-in. round baking pans.

Bake at 350° for 20-25 minutes or until a toothpick inserted near the center comes out clean. Cool for 10 minutes before removing from pans to wire racks to cool completely.

lemon poppy seed cake

apple nut cake with rum sauce

Chopping an ingredient before or after measuring it can make a difference in the outcome of the recipe. Here's a trick that might help you remember. If the word "chopped" comes before the ingredient when listed in a recipe, chop the ingredient before measuring. If the word "chopped" comes after the ingredient, chop after measuring. The cake pictured to the left calls for "1/2 cup chopped pecans," so chop them prior to measuring.

Bettie De Boeuf
Lawrenceville, Illinois
Special occasions call for wonderful recipes like this. The apples lend a fresh, fruity taste while the chopped pecans add a nice crunch. The simple-to-make rum sauce drizzled on top is the crowning touch on this tender cake.

apple nut cake with rum sauce

4   cups chopped peeled apples
2   cups sugar
2   eggs
1/2 cup canola oil
1   teaspoon almond extract
2   cups all-purpose flour
2   teaspoons baking powder
1   teaspoon salt
1   teaspoon ground cinnamon
1/2 cup chopped pecans
SAUCE:
1/2 cup butter, cubed
1   cup sugar
2   tablespoons all-purpose flour
1/8 teaspoon salt

1   cup water
2   teaspoons vanilla extract
1/2 teaspoon rum extract

In a large bowl, combine the chopped apples and sugar. Let stand for 30 minutes.

In a small bowl, whisk the eggs, oil and almond extract. Add to apple mixture and toss to coat. Combine the flour, baking powder, salt and cinnamon; stir into apple mixture just until moistened. Stir in pecans.

Transfer to a greased 11-in. x 7-in. baking dish. Bake at 350° for 35-40 minutes or until a toothpick inserted near the center comes out clean.

For sauce, in a small saucepan, melt butter. Stir in the sugar, flour and salt until smooth. Gradually add water. Bring to a boil; cook and stir for 2 minutes. Remove from the heat; stir in extracts. Serve with warm cake. **yield: 9 servings (2 cups sauce).**

truffle-topped cake

Taste of Home Test Kitchen • Greendale, Wisconsin
This eye-catching dessert created by our home economists will be the talk of the party—especially if guests find out how easy it is to make. Store-bought truffles and chopped hazelnuts add pizzazz to an ordinary boxed cake mix.

- 1 package (18-1/4 ounces) yellow cake mix
- 1 cup butter, softened
- 1 jar (12-1/4 ounces) caramel ice cream topping
- 3 tablespoons milk
- 1-1/2 teaspoons vanilla extract
- 6 cups confectioners' sugar
- 3/4 cup chopped hazelnuts

Assorted truffles

Prepare and bake cake according to package directions, using two greased 9-in. square baking pans. Cool for 10 minutes before removing from pans to wire racks to cool completely.

For frosting, in a large bowl, beat butter until light and fluffy. Beat in the caramel ice cream topping, milk and vanilla until smooth. Gradually add confectioners' sugar; beat until smooth.

Place one cake layer on a serving plate; spread with 1 cup frosting. Top with remaining cake layer. Frost top and sides of cake with remaining frosting. Press the hazelnuts into sides of cake. Top cake with truffles.
yield: 12 servings.

editor's note: This recipe was tested with Ferrero Rocher truffles.

truffle-topped cake

cherry-swirl chiffon cake

cherry-swirl chiffon cake

Edna Hoffman • Hebron, Indiana
This impressive-looking cake elicits oohs and ahhs whenever it appears on the table. Use peppermint extract in place of cherry extract if you desire.

- 8 egg whites
- 2-1/4 cups cake flour
- 1-1/2 cups sugar
- 3 teaspoons baking powder
- 1 teaspoon salt
- 5 egg yolks
- 3/4 cup water
- 1/2 cup canola oil
- 2 teaspoons cherry extract
- 1/2 teaspoon cream of tartar
- 6 drops red food coloring

FROSTING:
- 2/3 cup sugar
- 2 egg whites
- 1/3 cup light corn syrup
- 2 tablespoons plus 2 teaspoons water
- 1/4 teaspoon cream of tartar
- 1 teaspoon vanilla extract
- 1/2 teaspoon cherry extract
- 12 drops red food coloring

Crushed cherry hard candies, optional

Place egg whites in a large bowl; let stand at room temperature for 30 minutes. Meanwhile, in another large bowl, combine the flour, sugar, baking powder and salt. In a small bowl, whisk the egg yolks, water, oil and extract; add to the dry ingredients. Beat until well blended.

Add cream of tartar to egg whites; beat on medium speed until stiff peaks form. Fold into batter. Remove a third of the batter to a small bowl; tint pink with red food coloring.

Alternately spoon plain and pink batters into an ungreased 10-in. tube pan. Cut through batter with a knife to swirl.

Bake on the lowest oven rack at 325° for 60-70 minutes or until top springs back when lightly touched. Immediately invert the pan; cool completely, about 1 hour.

For frosting, in a small heavy saucepan, combine the sugar, egg whites, corn syrup, water and cream of tartar over low heat. With a hand mixer, beat on low speed for 1 minute. Continue beating on low over low heat until frosting reaches 160°, about 8-10 minutes. Pour into the bowl of a heavy-duty stand mixer; add the extracts. Beat on high until frosting forms stiff peaks, about 7 minutes.

Run a knife around sides and center tube of cake pan. Remove cake to a serving plate. Frost top and sides. Add drops of food coloring to frosting at base of cake; with a spatula, blend color up toward top of cake. Sprinkle with candies if desired. **yield: 12 servings.**

persimmon nut roll

Nancy Wilson • Van Nuys, California
For holiday gift-giving, I make a dozen or so of these rolls to share with friends and neighbors. They slice nicely straight from the freezer.

  3 **eggs**
  1 **cup sugar**
2/3 **cup mashed ripe persimmon pulp**
  1 **teaspoon lemon juice**
  1 **cup self-rising flour**
  2 **teaspoons ground cinnamon**
  1 **teaspoon baking powder**
  1 **teaspoon ground ginger**
1/2 **teaspoon salt**
1/2 **teaspoon ground nutmeg**
  1 **cup chopped pecans**
FILLING:
  1 **package (8 ounces) cream cheese, softened**
1/4 **cup butter, softened**
  1 **cup confectioners' sugar**

  1 **teaspoon vanilla extract**
Additional confectioners' sugar

Line a 15-in. x 10-in. x 1-in. baking pan with waxed paper and grease the paper; set aside. In a large bowl, beat eggs for 5 minutes on medium speed or until lemon-colored. Gradually add the sugar, persimmon pulp and lemon juice; beat for 3 minutes. Combine the flour, cinnamon, baking powder, ginger, salt and nutmeg; add to egg mixture and beat well.

Spread batter evenly in prepared pan; sprinkle with chopped pecans. Bake at 375° for 15 minutes or until lightly browned.

Cool in pan for 5 minutes. Turn cake onto a kitchen towel dusted with confectioners' sugar. Gently peel off waxed paper. Roll up cake in the towel jelly-roll style, starting with a short side. Cool completely on a wire rack.

For filling, in a small bowl, beat cream cheese and butter until smooth. Beat in the confectioners' sugar and vanilla until of spreading consistency.

Unroll cake and spread filling evenly over cake to within 1/2 in. of edges. Roll up again. Cover and refrigerate until serving. Dust with additional confectioners' sugar. Refrigerate or freeze leftovers. **yield: 10 servings.**

editor's note: To prepare persimmon pulp, puree the ripe seeded fruit (peeling is optional) in a blender or food processor, then strain through a sieve.

As a substitute for self-rising flour, place 1-1/2 teaspoons baking powder and 1/2 teaspoon salt in a measuring cup. Add all-purpose flour to measure 1 cup.

persimmon nut roll

cookies-and-cream cake

Pat Habiger • Spearville, Kansas
If you like cookies-and-cream ice cream, you'll love this cake.
Chocolate sandwich cookies are mixed into the batter and
pressed into the sweet and creamy frosting for a fun look.

1	package (18-1/4 ounces) white cake mix
1-1/4	cups water
1/3	cup canola oil
3	egg whites
1	cup coarsely crushed cream-filled chocolate sandwich cookies (about 8)

FROSTING:

1/2	cup shortening
4	to 4-1/2 cups confectioners' sugar
1/4	cup milk
1	teaspoon vanilla extract

Cream-filled chocolate sandwich cookies and crushed
cream-filled chocolate sandwich cookies, optional

In a large bowl, combine the cake mix, water, oil and
egg whites; beat on low speed for 30 seconds. Beat on
high for 2 minutes. Gently fold in crushed cookies.

Pour into two greased and floured 9-in. round baking
pans. Bake at 350° for 30-35 minutes or until a toothpick
inserted near the center comes out clean. Cool for
10 minutes before removing from pans to wire racks
to cool completely.

For frosting, beat the shortening, sugar, milk and vanilla
in another large bowl until smooth. Spread the frosting
between layers and over top and sides of cake.
Decorate the top with cookie and the sides with
crushed cookies if desired. **yield: 12 servings.**

creamy chocolate cake roll

Cathryn White • Newark, Delaware
The beauty of this recipe is that it looks elegant even though it's
so simple to make. It earns rave reviews, especially when
served with the chocolate raspberry sauce.

5	eggs, *separated*
1	cup confectioners' sugar
1	teaspoon vanilla extract
1/4	cup all-purpose flour
1/4	cup baking cocoa
2	tablespoons sugar

CREAM FILLING/FROSTING:

1	package (8 ounces) cream cheese, softened
1/3	cup sugar
1	package (3.4 ounces) instant vanilla pudding mix
1	teaspoon vanilla extract
4	cups heavy whipping cream

CHOCOLATE RASPBERRY SAUCE:

1-1/2	cups semisweet chocolate chips
1/2	cup seedless raspberry jam
1/4	cup heavy whipping cream
1	teaspoon almond extract

creamy chocolate cake roll

Place egg whites in a small bowl; let stand at room temperature for 30 minutes. Line a greased 15-in. x 10-in. x 1-in. baking pan with waxed paper; grease the paper and set aside.

In a large bowl, beat the egg yolks on high speed for 5 minutes or until thick and lemon-colored. Gradually beat in confectioners' sugar. Stir in vanilla. Sift flour and cocoa together twice; gradually add to yolk mixture and mix well (batter will be very thick).

Beat the egg whites on medium speed until soft peaks form. Gradually add sugar, 1 tablespoon at a time, beating on high until stiff peaks form. Gradually fold into batter. Spread evenly into prepared pan.

Bake at 375° for 12-15 minutes or until cake springs back when lightly touched. Cool for 5 minutes. Invert onto a kitchen towel dusted with baking cocoa. Gently peel off waxed paper. Roll up cake in the towel jelly-roll style, starting with a short side. Cool completely on a wire rack.

In a large bowl, beat the cream cheese, sugar and dry pudding mix until smooth. Beat in vanilla. Gradually beat in cream until thick.

Unroll cake; spread 2-1/2 cups filling evenly over cake to within 1/2 in. of edges. Roll up again. Place seam side down on a serving platter. Frost top, sides and ends with remaining filling. Cover and refrigerate for 1 hour.

In a small microwave-safe bowl, combine the chips, jam and cream. Microwave, uncovered, on high for 1-2 minutes or until smooth, stirring every 30 seconds. Stir in the extract. Serve with cake. Refrigerate leftovers. **yield: 10 servings.**

red, white & blue torte

Margery Bryan • Royal City, Washington
I have guests seeing fireworks when I turn frozen pound cake into a patriotic pleaser. Assemble this tempting torte early in the day and keep it in the refrigerator until it's time for dessert.

1	loaf (10-3/4 ounces) frozen pound cake, thawed
1/2	cup blueberry pie filling
1/2	cup strawberry *or* raspberry pie filling
1-3/4	cups whipped topping

Cut cake horizontally into three layers. Place bottom layer on a serving platter; spread with blueberry filling. Top with middle cake layer; spread with strawberry filling. Replace top of cake.

Frost top and sides with whipped topping. Refrigerate for several hours before slicing. **yield: 8 servings.**

orange angel food cake dessert

orange angel food cake dessert

Janet Springer • St. Petersburg, Florida
Light-as-air angel food cake, sugar-free orange gelatin and sugar-free vanilla pudding help cut the fat and calories from this sunny citrus dessert that I frequently make for family and friends.

1	package (16 ounces) angel food cake mix
1	package (.3 ounce) sugar-free orange gelatin
3/4	cup boiling water
1/2	cup cold water
1-1/2	cups cold fat-free milk
1	package (1 ounce) sugar-free instant vanilla pudding mix
1	teaspoon orange extract
1	carton (8 ounces) frozen reduced-fat whipped topping, thawed
1	small navel orange, halved and sliced
1/2	cup sliced almonds, toasted

Prepare and bake cake according to package directions, using an ungreased 10-in. tube pan. Immediately invert tube pan; cool completely.

In a small bowl, dissolve gelatin in boiling water; stir in cold water and set aside. Cut cake into 2-in. slices; arrange cake slices in a ungreased 13-in. x 9-in. dish. With a meat fork, poke holes about 2 in. apart into the cake. Slowly pour gelatin over cake; chill until set.

In a large bowl, whisk milk and pudding mix for 2 minutes. Whisk in extract. Let stand for 2 minutes or until soft-set. Fold in whipped topping. Spread over cake. Garnish with orange slices and almonds. Cover and refrigerate until serving. **yield: 15 servings.**

black forest cheesecake

Carey Lynn Enns
Aylmer, Ontario
This dessert puts a delicious spin on the classic black forest cake. Top each serving with canned cherry pie filling, a dollop of whipped cream and chocolate curls for an elegant presentation.

black forest cheesecake

   2   packages (8 ounces *each*) cream cheese, softened
3/4   cup sugar
   2   eggs, lightly beaten
   1   teaspoon vanilla extract
1/2   teaspoon almond extract
Dash salt
BATTER:
1-1/2   cups sugar
1/2   cup canola oil
   1   egg
1-1/2   teaspoons vanilla extract
2-1/4   cups all-purpose flour
1/3   cup baking cocoa
   1   teaspoon baking soda
1/2   teaspoon baking powder
1/4   teaspoon salt
1-1/2   cups buttermilk *or* sour cream

TOPPING:
   1   can (21 ounces) cherry pie filling
Whipped topping and chocolate curls, optional

In a large bowl, beat cream cheese and sugar until smooth. Add the eggs; beat on low speed just until combined. Stir in extracts and salt; set aside.

In another large bowl, beat the sugar, oil, egg and vanilla until well blended. Combine the flour, cocoa, baking soda, baking powder and salt; gradually add to sugar mixture alternately with buttermilk.

Spoon half of the batter into a greased and floured 10-in. fluted tube pan; spread with half of the cream cheese mixture. Repeat layers.

Bake at 375° for 45-50 minutes or until a knife inserted near the center comes out clean. Cool for 10 minutes before removing from pan to a wire rack to cool completely.

Slice cake; serve with pie filling. Garnish with whipped topping and chocolate curls if desired. Refrigerate leftovers. **yield: 12 servings.**

buttermilk pound cake

Gracie Hanchey • De Ridder, Louisiana

This cake is the one I make most often. It is a genuine Southern recipe and one I personally think can't be topped. Once people taste it, they'll request the recipe.

1	cup butter
3	cups sugar
4	eggs
3	cups all-purpose flour
1/4	teaspoon baking soda
1	cup buttermilk
1	teaspoon vanilla extract

Confectioners' sugar, optional

In a large bowl, cream butter and sugar until light and fluffy. Add eggs, one at a time, beating well after each addition. Combine flour and baking soda; add alternately with the buttermilk and beat well. Stir in vanilla.

Pour into a greased and floured 10-in. fluted tube pan. Bake at 325° for 70 minutes or until a toothpick inserted near the center comes out clean. Cool in pan for 15 minutes before removing to a wire rack to cool completely. Dust with confectioners' sugar if desired. **yield: 16-20 servings.**

dobostorte

Susan Carn • Fremont, Ohio

It takes some time to prepare Dobostorte, but the effort is well worth it! Every forkful of this traditional seven-layer Hungarian cake is moist and delicious.

6	eggs, *separated*
3/4	cup sugar
1	cup all-purpose flour

CHOCOLATE BUTTERCREAM:

1-3/4	cups semisweet chocolate chips
1/3	cup plus 2 tablespoons brewed coffee
1/3	cup plus 2 tablespoons sugar
7	egg yolks, lightly beaten
1-1/4	teaspoons vanilla extract
1	cup butter, softened

CARAMEL TOPPING:

12	caramels
7	teaspoons evaporated milk

Place the egg whites in a small bowl; let stand at room temperature for 30 minutes. Meanwhile, using a pencil, draw an 8-in. circle on each of seven sheets of parchment paper. Place each sheet, pencil mark down, on a baking sheet; set aside.

In a large bowl, beat the egg yolks on high speed for 5 minutes or until thick and lemon-colored. Gradually beat in sugar. Sift flour twice; gradually add to yolk mixture and mix well (batter will be very thick).

With clean beaters, beat egg whites on medium until soft peaks form. Gradually fold into batter. Place 1/2 cup batter on one of the prepared baking sheets; using a small spatula, spread batter evenly into an 8-in. circle. Bake at 350° for 6-7 minutes or until cake springs back when lightly touched (do not overbake).

Cool on a wire for 5 minutes; gently peel off parchment paper. Repeat with remaining batter and pans. When cool, stack cakes with waxed paper or paper towels in between. Gently smooth the top and sides of stack. Refrigerate overnight if desired.

For buttercream, in a small saucepan, melt chips with coffee and sugar; stir until smooth. Remove from the heat. Add a small amount of mixture to egg yolks; return all to the pan, stirring constantly. Cook for 2 minutes or until mixture is thickened and reaches 160°, stirring constantly. Remove from the heat; stir in vanilla. Cool to room temperature.

In a large bowl with a whisk attachment, beat butter until fluffy, about 5 minutes. Gradually beat in chocolate mixture. If necessary, refrigerate until frosting achieves spreading consistency.

Set aside one cake layer. Spread 1/4 cup frosting on each of the remaining cake layers; stack on a serving plate.

In a small saucepan, melt caramels with milk. Remove from the heat; pour evenly over reserved cake layer. Place on top of cake. Frost sides of cake and decorate the top with remaining frosting. **yield: 12 servings.**

dobostorte

raspberry butter torte

raspberry butter torte

Taste of Home Test Kitchen • Greendale, Wisconsin
Raspberry pie filling and homemade chocolate frosting jazz up a packaged cake mix in this picture-perfect torte created by our Test Kitchen. With a hint of rum flavor, it's rich and creamy for special occasions, but so simple to make, you could prepare it on weeknights, too.

    1   package (18-1/2 ounces) butter recipe golden cake mix
  1/4   cup chopped almonds, toasted
    2   cups heavy whipping cream
    1   cup confectioners' sugar
  1/4   cup baking cocoa
1-1/2   teaspoons rum extract
    2   cups raspberry filling
Chocolate curls
Sliced almonds, toasted, optional

Prepare cake batter according to package directions; fold in chopped almonds. Pour into two greased and floured 9-in. round baking pans. Bake as directed. Cool for 10 minutes before removing from pans to wire racks to cool completely.

For frosting, in a small bowl, beat cream until it begins to thicken. Add the confectioners' sugar, cocoa and extract; beat until stiff peaks form.

Cut each cake into two horizontal layers. Place one layer on a serving plate; spread with 1/2 cup raspberry filling

and 1/2 cup frosting. Repeat with remaining cake layers.

Place remaining frosting in a pastry bag with a #195 star tip. Decorate top and sides of cake as desired. Garnish with chocolate curls. Sprinkle with sliced almonds if desired. Store in the refrigerator. **yield: 12-14 servings.**

editor's note: For the cake pictured at left, pipe about 1/2 cup frosting around the cake between the layers and 1-1/2 cups on top.

sweet potato cake

Wanda Rolen • Sevierville, Tennessee
Just like my mom, I love to cook. This sweet cake is perfect for church potlucks, homecoming parties or even as the finishing touch to any special meal.

    1   cup canola oil
    2   cups sugar
    4   eggs
1-1/2   cups finely shredded uncooked sweet potato (about 1 medium)
  1/4   cup hot water
    1   teaspoon vanilla extract
2-1/2   cups self-rising flour
    1   teaspoon ground cinnamon
    1   cup sliced almonds
FROSTING:
  1/2   cup butter, cubed
    1   cup packed brown sugar
    1   cup evaporated milk
    3   egg yolks, lightly beaten

sweet potato cake

1-1/2 cups flaked coconut
1 cup sliced almonds
1 teaspoon vanilla extract

In a large bowl, beat oil and sugar. Add eggs, one at a time, beating well after each addition. Beat in the sweet potato, water and vanilla. Combine flour and cinnamon; gradually add to potato mixture until well blended. Stir in almonds.

Pour into a greased 13-in. x 9-in. baking pan. Bake at 350° for 40-45 minutes or until a toothpick inserted near the center comes out clean.

For frosting, melt butter in a saucepan; whisk in the brown sugar, milk and egg yolks until smooth. Cook and stir over medium heat until mixture reaches at least 160° and coats the back of a metal spoon. Remove from the heat; stir in coconut, almonds and vanilla. Spread over warm cake. Cool on a wire rack. **yield: 12-15 servings.**

---

editor's note: As a substitute for each cup of self-rising flour, place 1-1/2 teaspoons baking powder and 1/2 teaspoon salt in a measuring cup. Add all-purpose flour to measure 1 cup.

grandma's blackberry cake

Diana Martin • Moundsville, West Virginia
My grandmother made this lightly seasoned spice cake with her mother, and it's been passed down to five generations in our family. The wonderful flavor of blackberries comes through in every bite.

---

1 cup fresh blackberries
2 cups all-purpose flour, *divided*
1/2 cup butter, softened
1 cup sugar
2 eggs
1 teaspoon baking soda
1 teaspoon ground cinnamon
1 teaspoon ground nutmeg
1/2 teaspoon salt
1/4 teaspoon ground cloves
1/4 teaspoon ground allspice
3/4 cup buttermilk
Whipped cream, optional

Toss blackberries with 2 tablespoons of flour; set aside. In a large bowl, cream butter and sugar until light and fluffy. Beat in eggs. Combine the baking soda, cinnamon, nutmeg, salt, cloves, allspice and remaining flour; add to creamed mixture alternately with buttermilk, beating well after each addition. Fold in blackberries.

grandma's blackberry cake

Pour into a greased and floured 9-in. square baking pan. Bake at 350° for 45-50 minutes or until a toothpick inserted near the center comes out clean. Cool on a wire rack. Serve with whipped cream if desired. **yield: 9 servings.**

million-dollar pound cake

George Dunn • Jasper, Texas
We've always included cake on our family menus throughout the years, and the recipe for this pound cake is a favorite! It has a very fine texture that makes it unusually smooth. That texture, plus fantastic flavor, makes this a special treat each time we serve it.

---

2 cups butter, softened
3 cups sugar
6 eggs
1 teaspoon almond extract
1 teaspoon vanilla extract
4 cups all-purpose flour
3/4 cup milk

In a large bowl, cream butter and sugar until light and fluffy. Add eggs, one at a time, beating well after each addition. Beat in extracts. Gradually add flour to creamed mixture alternately with milk, just until blended. Pour batter into a greased and floured 10-in. tube pan.

Bake at 325° for about 1 hour and 40 minutes or until a toothpick inserted near the center comes out clean.

Cool for 15 minutes before removing from pan to a wire rack to cool completely. **yield: 16 servings.**

lemonade layer cake

Jana Randich • Phoenix, Arizona
The lemonade concentrate called for in this recipe gives both the cake and frosting fantastic flavor. Garnish this dessert with lemon slices and mint leaves for an elegant look.

    6   tablespoons butter, softened
1-1/3   cups sugar
    3   tablespoons lemonade concentrate
    2   tablespoons grated lemon peel
    2   teaspoons vanilla extract
    2   eggs
    2   egg whites
    2   cups all-purpose flour
    1   teaspoon baking powder
  1/2   teaspoon baking soda
  1/4   teaspoon salt
1-1/4   cups 1% buttermilk
FROSTING:
    1   package (8 ounces) reduced-fat cream cheese
    2   tablespoons butter, softened
    2   tablespoons grated lemon peel
    2   teaspoons lemonade concentrate
    1   teaspoon vanilla extract
3-1/2   cups confectioners' sugar

In a large bowl, beat butter and sugar until crumbly, about 2 minutes. Add the lemonade concentrate, lemon peel and vanilla; mix well. Add eggs and egg whites, one at a time, beating well after each addition.

Combine the flour, baking powder, baking soda and salt. Add to the butter mixture alternately with buttermilk.

Coat two 9-in. round baking pans with cooking spray and dust with flour. Pour batter to prepared pans.

Bake at 350° for 18-22 minutes or until a toothpick inserted near the center comes out clean. Cool for 10 minutes before removing from pans to a wire rack to cool completely.

For frosting, in a small bowl, combine cream cheese and butter until smooth. Add the lemon peel, lemonade concentrate and vanilla; mix well. Gradually beat in confectioners' sugar until smooth. Spread frosting between layers and over top and sides of cake. Refrigerate for at least 1 hour before serving. Refrigerate leftovers. **yield: 16 servings.**

cheese-swirl chocolate cake

Jennifer Bangerter • Warrensburg, Missouri
I recently made this moist chocolate cake for my sister and her husband. I've never seen cake disappear so quickly! The swirls of cream cheese are divine, and it's great with or without the pretty strawberry sauce.

    1   package (8 ounces) cream cheese, softened
    4   eggs
  1/4   cup sugar
  1/2   teaspoon vanilla extract
    1   package (18-1/4 ounces) devil's food cake mix
1-1/4   cups water
  1/2   cup canola oil
    1   package (10 ounces) frozen sweetened sliced strawberries, thawed

In a small bowl, combine the cream cheese, 1 egg, sugar and vanilla; set aside. In a large bowl, combine the cake mix, water, oil and remaining eggs. Beat on low speed for 30 seconds; beat on medium for 2 minutes.

Pour half of the batter into a greased 13-in. x 9-in. baking pan. Drop half of the cream cheese mixture by tablespoonfuls over the batter. Repeat layers. Cut through the batter with a knife to swirl the cream cheese mixture.

Bake at 350°; for 35-40 minutes or until a toothpick inserted near the center comes out clean (cake may crack). Cool on a wire rack.

Meanwhile, in a blender, cover and process strawberries until pureed. Serve with cake. **yield: 12 servings.**

lemonade layer cake

midsummer sponge cake

midsummer sponge cake

Robin Fuhrman • Fond du Lac, Wisconsin
You are sure to love everything about this beautiful seasonal dessert—the tender cake layers, fluffy cream filling and glazed fresh fruit topping.

4	eggs
1-1/4	cups sugar
1-1/4	cups all-purpose flour
2	teaspoons baking powder
1/2	cup water
1-1/2	cups cold milk
1/2	teaspoon vanilla extract
1	package (3.4 ounces) instant vanilla pudding mix
2	cups whipped topping
3	tablespoons lemon gelatin
1/2	cup boiling water

Assorted fresh fruit

In a large bowl, beat eggs until light and fluffy. Gradually beat in sugar until light and lemon-colored. Combine flour and baking powder; add to egg mixture alternately with water, beating just until smooth. Pour into a greased and floured 10-in. springform pan.

Bake at 375° for 20-25 minutes or until cake springs back when lightly touched. Cool on a wire rack for 1 hour.

Carefully run a knife around edge of the pan; remove sides. Invert onto a wire rack. Remove bottom of pan; invert cake so the top is up. For filling, in a large bowl, whisk the milk, vanilla and pudding mix for 2 minutes or until thickened; chill for 10 minutes. Fold in the whipped topping.

For glaze, dissolve gelatin in boiling water. Add enough cold water to measure 1 cup. Chill for 15 minutes or until slightly thickened.

Cut cake in half horizontally. Place bottom layer on a serving plate. Spread filling over cake layer; top with second cake layer and fruit. Drizzle with glaze. Chill until serving. **yield: 10-12 servings.**

coconut cake supreme

Betty Claycomb • Alverton, Pennsylvania
I make most cakes from scratch, but during the holiday rush, this easy-to-make recipe buys me some time. Most eager eaters don't suspect the box-mix shortcut once I dress up the cake with coconut filling and frosting.

1	package (18-1/4 ounces) yellow cake mix
2	cups (16 ounces) sour cream
2	cups sugar
1-1/2	cups flaked coconut
1	carton (8 ounces) frozen whipped topping, thawed

Fresh mint leaves and red gumdrops, optional

Prepare and bake cake according to package directions using two 9-in. round baking pans. Cool cakes in pans for 10 minutes before removing to wire racks to cool completely.

For filling, in a large bowl, combine sour cream and sugar. Stir in coconut (filling will be soft). Set aside 1 cup of filling for frosting.

Cut each cake horizontally into two layers. Place bottom layer on a serving plate; top with a third of the filling. Repeat layers twice. Top with the remaining cake layer.

Fold reserved filling into whipped topping; frost cake. Refrigerate for at least 4 hours. Garnish with mint and gumdrops if desired. **yield: 10-12 servings.**

coconut cake supreme

perfect pastries

blueberry streusel coffee cake, p. 74

Rich, delicate, *filled with cream or rolled in sugar, there's simply nothing like the blissful, old-fashioned comfort of made-at-home bakery pleasures. Here, you'll find a heavenly lineup of cream puffs, crepes, coffee cakes, eclairs and other pastry perfections that are just as fabulous for dessert as they are for brunch. The from-scratch goodness of these traditional favorites will leave hungry tummies more than satisfied.*

chocolate eclairs

chocolate eclairs

Janet Davis • Murfreesboro, Tennessee
I won the grand prize with this recipe at a Chocolate Lovers Cook-Off contest in our town. This is one of my most-requested desserts.

1/2	cup butter, cubed
1	cup water
1	cup all-purpose flour
1/4	teaspoon salt
4	eggs

FILLING:

2-1/2	cups cold milk
1	package (5.1 ounces) instant vanilla pudding mix
1	cup heavy whipping cream
1/4	cup confectioners' sugar
1	teaspoon vanilla extract

CHOCOLATE ICING:

2	squares (1 ounce *each*) semisweet chocolate
2	tablespoons butter
1	cup confectioners' sugar
2	to 3 tablespoons hot water

In a large saucepan, combine butter and water. Bring to a rapid boil, stirring until the butter melts. Reduce heat to low; add flour and salt. Stir vigorously until mixture leaves the sides of the pan and forms a stiff ball. Remove from the heat. Add eggs, one at a time, beating well after each addition.

With a tablespoon or a pastry tube fitting with a #10 or larger tip, spoon or pipe the dough into 4-in.-long x 1-1/2-in.-wide strips on a greased baking sheet.

Bake at 450° for 15 minutes. Reduce heat to 325°; bake 20 minutes longer. Cool on a wire rack.

For filling, in a large bowl, whisk milk and pudding mix for 2 minutes. Let stand for 2 minutes or until soft-set. In another large bowl, whip cream until soft peaks form. Beat in sugar and vanilla; fold into pudding. Fill cooled shells. (Chill remaining pudding mixture for another use.)

For icing, melt the chocolate and butter in a small saucepan over low heat. Stir in sugar. Add hot water until icing is smooth and reaches desired consistency. Cool slightly. Spread icing over eclairs. Chill until serving. **yield: 8-9 servings.**

mixed berry pizza

Gretchen Widner • Sun City West, Arizona
The fresh fruit shines through in this colorful dessert pizza. It's also a tempting appetizer at parties because it's a sweet change of pace from the usual savory dips.

1	tube (8 ounces) refrigerated reduced-fat crescent rolls
11	ounces reduced-fat cream cheese
1/2	cup apricot preserves
2	tablespoons confectioners' sugar
2	cups sliced fresh strawberries
1	cup fresh blueberries
1	cup fresh raspberries

Unroll crescent roll dough and place in a 15-in. x 10-in. x 1-in. baking pan coated with cooking spray. Press onto the bottom and 1 in. up the sides of pan to form a crust; seal seams and perforations. Bake at 375° for 8-10 minutes or until golden. Cool completely.

In a large bowl, beat cream cheese until smooth. Beat in the preserves and confectioners' sugar; spread over crust. Cover and refrigerate for 1-2 hours.

Just before serving, arrange berries on top. Cut into 20 pieces. **yield: 20 servings.**

mixed berry pizza

chocolate crepes

DESSERT *Tip*

Try this easy substitution if you don't have any half-and-half cream on hand. For dishes that are cooked or baked, you may substitute 4-1/2 teaspoons melted butter plus enough whole milk to equal 1 cup. One cup of evaporated milk may also be substituted for each cup of half-and-half cream.

Taste of Home
Test Kitchen
Greendale, Wisconsin
If you think crepes are merely breakfast fare, we insist you try these cream-filled chocolate crepes for dessert!

chocolate crepes

1-1/2 cups milk
   3 eggs
   3 tablespoons water
   2 tablespoons canola oil
1-1/2 teaspoons vanilla extract
1-1/2 cups all-purpose flour
  1/4 cup sugar
  1/4 cup baking cocoa
  1/8 teaspoon salt

FILLING:
   1 package (8 ounces) cream cheese, softened
  1/4 cup sugar
  1/2 cup sour cream
  1/2 teaspoon vanilla extract
  1/3 cup creme de cacao
   1 carton (8 ounces) frozen whipped topping, thawed

FUDGE SAUCE:
  3/4 cup semisweet chocolate chips

  1/4 cup butter
  1/2 cup sugar
  2/3 cup half-and-half cream
  10 mint Andes candies, chopped, optional

For batter, place the first nine ingredients in a blender or food processor. Cover and process until smooth. Refrigerate for 1 hour.

Meanwhile, in a large bowl, beat cream cheese and sugar until light and fluffy. Beat in sour cream and vanilla. Fold in creme de cacao and whipped topping. Cover and refrigerate for at least 1 hour.

For the fudge sauce, in a large saucepan, melt chocolate chips and butter over low heat. Stir in sugar and cream. Bring to a boil. Reduce heat; simmer, uncovered, for 10 minutes. Set aside and keep warm.

Heat a lightly greased 8-in. nonstick skillet; pour 2 tablespoons batter into center of skillet. Lift and tilt pan to evenly coat bottom. Cook until top appears dry; turn and cook 15-20 seconds longer. Remove to a wire rack. Repeat with remaining batter, greasing skillet as needed. When cool, stack crepes with waxed paper or paper towels in between.

Spoon 1/4 cup filling down the center of each crepe; roll up. Top with fudge sauce. Sprinkle with mint candies if desired. **yield: 10 servings.**

county fair funnel cakes

Taste of Home Test Kitchen • Greendale, Wisconsin
What would a county fair be without these delicious deep-fried pastries? To make these timeless treats, slowly swirl the batter into oil, brown it to perfection and lightly dust with a sprinkling of confectioners' sugar.

2	eggs, lightly beaten
1-1/2	cups milk
1/4	cup packed brown sugar
2	cups all-purpose flour
1-1/2	teaspoons baking powder
1/4	teaspoon salt

Oil for deep-fat frying
Confectioners' sugar

In a large bowl, combine the eggs, milk and brown sugar. Combine flour, baking powder and salt; beat into egg mixture until smooth.

In an electric skillet or deep-fat fryer, heat oil to 375°. Cover the bottom of a funnel spout with your finger; ladle 1/2 cup batter into funnel. Holding the funnel several inches above the skillet, release finger and move funnel in a spiral motion until all of the batter is released (scraping funnel with a rubber spatula if needed).

Fry for 2 minutes on each side or until golden brown. Drain on paper towels. Repeat with remaining batter. Dust funnel cakes with confectioners' sugar; serve warm. **yield: 6 servings.**

editor's note: The batter can be poured from a liquid measuring cup instead of a funnel.

county fair funnel cakes

cream puff dessert

cream puff dessert

Lisa Nash • Blaine, Minnesota
Instead of making individual cream puffs, make this rich dessert with a cream puff base and sweet toppings.

1	cup water
1/2	cup butter
1	cup all-purpose flour
4	eggs

FILLING:

1	package (8 ounces) cream cheese, softened
3-1/2	cups cold milk
2	packages (3.9 ounces *each*) instant chocolate pudding mix

TOPPING:

1	carton (8 ounces) frozen whipped topping, thawed
1/4	cup chocolate ice cream topping
1/4	cup caramel ice cream topping
1/3	cup chopped almonds

In a large saucepan, bring the water and butter to a boil over medium heat. Add flour all at once; stir until a smooth ball forms. Remove from the heat; let stand for 5 minutes. Add the eggs, one at a time, beating well after each addition. Continue beating until mixture is smooth and shiny.

Spread into a greased 13-in. x 9-in. baking dish. Bake at 400° for 30-35 minutes or until puffed and golden brown. Remove to a wire rack to cool completely.

For filling, beat the cream cheese, milk and pudding mix in a large bowl until smooth. Spread over puff; refrigerate for 20 minutes.

Spread with whipped topping; refrigerate until serving. Drizzle with the chocolate and caramel ice cream toppings; sprinkle with almonds. Refrigerate leftovers. **yield: 12 servings.**

apple strudel

Helen Lesh • Forsyth, Missouri
This is one of my favorite recipes for autumn celebrations and holiday meals. The aroma of this dessert baking on a cool, crisp day is absolutely wonderful.

mocha cream puffs

1	cup cold butter, cubed
2	cups all-purpose flour
1	cup (8 ounces) sour cream
1/4	teaspoon salt

FILLING:

2	cups dry bread crumbs
1/4	cup butter, melted
4	medium baking apples, peeled and chopped
2	cups sugar
1	cup golden raisins
1/2	cup chopped pecans
2	teaspoons ground cinnamon

Confectioners' sugar, optional

In a large bowl, cut butter into flour until mixture resembles coarse crumbs. Stir in sour cream and salt. Shape the dough into a ball; cover and refrigerate overnight.

For filling, combine bread crumbs and butter. Add the apples, sugar, raisins, pecans and cinnamon, set aside. Divide dough into thirds; turn onto a floured surface. Roll each into a 15-in. x 12-in. rectangle. Spoon filling evenly onto dough; spread to within 1 in. of edges. Roll up from one long side; pinch seams and ends to seal.

Carefully place each loaf seam side down on an ungreased baking sheet. Bake at 350° for 55-60 minutes or until light brown. Cool completely on wire racks. Dust with confectioners' sugar if desired. **yield: 3 loaves.**

mocha cream puffs

Aimee Kirk • Jacksonville, Alabama
Looking for a special-occasion dessert that's easy to fix? Try these golden puffs with a chocolaty filling. They're a taste sensation, yet you won't have to worry about storing several of them in your refrigerator.

1/4	cup water
2	tablespoons butter
1/8	teaspoon salt
1/4	cup all-purpose flour
1	egg

FILLING:

2/3	cup heavy whipping cream, *divided*
3	tablespoons semisweet chocolate chips
2	teaspoons sugar

Dash salt

1/2	teaspoon vanilla extract
1/2	teaspoon instant coffee granules

Confectioners' sugar

In a small saucepan, bring the water, butter and salt to a boil. Add flour at once and stir until a smooth ball forms. Remove from the heat; let stand for 5 minutes. Add egg; beat until mixture is smooth and shiny.

Drop batter into four mounds 3 in. apart on a greased baking sheet. Bake at 425° for 20-25 minutes or until golden brown. Remove puffs to a wire rack. Immediately split puffs open; remove tops and set aside. Discard soft dough from inside. Cool puffs.

For the filling, in a small saucepan, combine 3 tablespoons cream, chocolate chips, sugar and salt. Cook over low heat until the chips are melted; stir until blended. Remove from the heat; gradually stir in the vanilla, coffee and remaining cream.

Transfer to a small bowl. Refrigerate until chilled. Beat filling until stiff. Fill cream puffs just before serving; replace tops. Dust with confectioners' sugar. **yield: 4 cream puffs.**

cherry rhubarb coffee cake

mixture resembles fine crumbs. In a small bowl, beat the buttermilk, eggs and vanilla. Add to flour mixture; stir just until moistened.

Spread a little more than half of the batter into a greased 13-in. x 9-in. baking pan. Spread cooled filling over batter. Drop remaining batter by teaspoonfuls onto filling.

For topping, combine sugar and flour. Cut in butter until mixture forms coarse crumbs. Sprinkle over batter. Bake at 350° for 40-45 minutes. **yield: 16-20 servings.**

editor's note: If using frozen rhubarb, measure rhubarb while still frozen, then thaw completely. Drain in a colander, but do not press liquid out.

cherry rhubarb coffee cake

Kenneth Jacques • Hemet, California
I'm retired now, but when I was working I made this coffee cake for co-workers and also a men's Bible study class. I changed the original recipe from a strawberry/rhubarb combination to one with cherry, which I think gives it a richer flavor.

 4 cups chopped fresh *or* frozen rhubarb
 2 tablespoons lemon juice
 1 cup sugar
 1/3 cup cornstarch
 1 can (20 ounces) cherry pie filling
CAKE:
 3 cups all-purpose flour
 1 cup sugar
 1 teaspoon baking powder
 1 teaspoon baking soda
 1/2 teaspoon salt
 1 cup cold butter, cubed
 1 cup buttermilk
 2 eggs, lightly beaten
 1 teaspoon vanilla extract
CRUMB TOPPING:
1-1/2 cups sugar
 1 cup all-purpose flour
 1/2 cup cold butter, cubed

In a saucepan, cook rhubarb and lemon juice over medium-low heat for 5 minutes, stirring often to prevent burning. Combine sugar and cornstarch; add to rhubarb mixture. Cook and stir 5 minutes more until thickened and bubbly. Stir in pie filling; set aside to cool.

For cake, combine the flour, sugar, baking powder, baking soda and salt in a large bowl. Cut in butter until

long johns

Twilla Eisele • Wellsville, Kansas
The tattered recipe in my files is a good indication of how popular these doughnuts have been in our family over the years. They disappear in a hurry, so I typically double the recipe to make an extra batch.

 1 package (1/4 ounce) active dry yeast
 1/4 cup warm water (110° to 115°)
 1 cup warm milk (110° to 115°)
 1/4 cup butter, softened
 1/4 cup sugar
 1/2 teaspoon salt
 1 egg
3-1/4 to 3-3/4 cups all-purpose flour
Oil for deep-fat frying
GLAZE:
1-1/4 cups confectioners' sugar

long johns

1 tablespoon brown sugar
1 tablespoon water
1/2 teaspoon vanilla extract
1/8 teaspoon salt

In a large bowl, dissolve yeast in warm water. Add the milk, butter, sugar, salt and egg and 2 cups flour. Beat until smooth. Stir in enough flour to form a soft dough.

Do not knead. Place in a greased bowl, turning once to grease top. Cover and let rise in a warm place until doubled, about 1 hour.

Punch dough down. Turn onto a lightly floured surface; roll into a 12-in. x 8-in. rectangle. Cut into 3-in. x 1-in. rectangles. Place dough on greased baking sheets. Cover and let rise in a warm place until doubled, about 30 minutes.

In an electric skillet or deep-fat fryer, heat oil to 400°. Fry doughnuts, a few at a time, until golden brown on both sides. Drain on paper towels. Combine glaze ingredients. Dip tops of doughnuts in glaze while warm. **yield: 2-1/2 dozen.**

blue-ribbon doughnuts

Kay McEwen • Sussex, New Brunswick
I'm the proud grandmother of 16 grandchildren, and this doughnut recipe is one of their all-time favorite treats. They can't seem to get enough of these tasty delights, and they love to cut them out for Grandma to fry.

6 to 7 cups all-purpose flour
2 cups sugar
4 teaspoons cream of tartar
2 teaspoons baking soda
1 teaspoon salt
1 teaspoon ground nutmeg
3 eggs
1 cup milk
1 cup heavy whipping cream
1 teaspoon vanilla extract
Oil for deep-fat frying

In a large bowl, combine 4-1/2 cups flour, sugar, baking powder and salt. Combine the eggs, milk, oil, orange juice and peel; stir into dry ingredients just until moistened. Stir in enough remaining flour to form a soft dough.

Turn onto a floured surface; knead until smooth, about 8-10 minutes. Place in a greased bowl, turning once to grease top. Cover and refrigerate for 2-3 hours.

On a floured surface, roll dough to 1/2-in. thickness.

Cut with a lightly floured 1/2-in. doughnut cutter.

In an electric skillet or deep-fat fryer, heat oil to 375°. Fry doughnuts, a few at a time, for 2 minutes on each side or until browned. Drain doughnuts on paper towels. **yield: 3 dozen.**

chocolate napoleons

Roberta Strohmaier • Lebanon, New Jersey
People will think you fussed over these impressive desserts. I use frozen puff pastry for the flaky shells and dress up pudding mix for the yummy chocolate filling.

1 sheet frozen puff pastry, thawed
2 cups cold milk
2 cups (16 ounces) sour cream
2 packages (3.9 ounces *each*) instant chocolate pudding mix
TOPPING:
1 cup confectioners' sugar
2 tablespoons milk
2 squares (1 ounce *each*) semisweet chocolate, melted and cooled

On a lightly floured surface, roll pastry into a 12-in. square. Cut into twelve 4-in. x 3-in. rectangles. Place on ungreased baking sheets. Bake at 400° for 9-12 minutes or until puffed and golden brown. Remove to wire racks to cool.

In a small bowl, whisk milk and sour cream until smooth. Add pudding mix; whisk for 2 minutes or until blended. Refrigerate for 5 minutes.

To assemble, split each pastry in half. Spoon pudding mixture over bottom halves and replace tops. Combine confectioners' sugar and milk until smooth; drizzle over top. Drizzle with melted chocolate. Serve immediately. **yield: 12 servings.**

chocolate napoleons

blueberry streusel coffee cake

Eunice Sawatzky
Lowe Farm, Manitoba
My sister-in-law made this delicious coffee cake with the fresh blueberries we picked while our families were vacationing at her cottage one summer. I've also used frozen berries with wonderful results. Each time I bake this bread, we're reminded of those good times.

blueberry streusel coffee cake

1/2	**cup butter, softened**
1-3/4	**cups sugar**
2	**eggs**
2	**teaspoons vanilla extract**
3-1/2	**cups all-purpose flour**
2	**tablespoons baking powder**
1	**teaspoon salt**
1-1/2	**cups milk**
3	**cups fresh or frozen blueberries**

STREUSEL TOPPING:

3/4	**cup sugar**
1/2	**teaspoon ground cinnamon**
1/3	**cup cold butter**

In a large bowl, cream butter and sugar until light and fluffy. Beat in eggs and vanilla until blended. Combine the flour, baking powder and salt; add to creamed mixture alternately with milk, beating well after each addition. Fold in blueberries.

Pour into a greased 13-in. x 9-in. baking dish. For topping, combine sugar and cinnamon. Cut in butter until mixture resembles coarse crumbs. Sprinkle over batter.

Bake at 375° for 35-40 minutes or until a toothpick inserted near the center comes out clean. Cool coffee cake in pan on a wire rack. **yield: 12-16 servings.**

editor's note: If using frozen blueberries, do not thaw before adding to the batter.

cranberry coffee cake

Doris Brearley • Vestal, New York

A former neighbor gave me this classic coffee cake recipe. The yummy cake relies on baking mix, canned cranberry sauce and an easy nut topping, so it's truly a quick bread.

- 2   cups biscuit/baking mix
- 2   tablespoons sugar
- 2/3 cup milk
- 1   egg, lightly beaten
- 2/3 cup jellied cranberry sauce

TOPPING:
- 1/2 cup chopped walnuts
- 1/2 cup packed brown sugar
- 1/2 teaspoon ground cinnamon

GLAZE:
- 1   cup confectioners' sugar
- 2   tablespoons milk
- 1/4 teaspoon vanilla extract

In a large bowl, combine the biscuit mix, sugar, milk and egg. Pour into a greased 8-in. square baking dish. Drop cranberry sauce by teaspoonfuls over batter. Combine topping ingredients; sprinkle over cranberry sauce. Bake at 400° for 18-23 minutes or until a toothpick inserted near the center comes out clean. Cool on a wire rack.

In a small bowl, combine the glaze ingredients; drizzle over coffee cake. **yield: 9 servings.**

cranberry coffee cake

almond pear tartlets

almond pear tartlets

Marie Rizzio • Traverse City, Michigan

Although they're quick to fix, you'll want to savor these pretty pastries slowly. An almond sauce and a crispy crust complement these delicately spiced pears.

- 1   egg, lightly beaten
- 1/2 cup plus 6 tablespoons sugar, *divided*
- 3/4 cup heavy whipping cream
- 2   tablespoons butter, melted
- 1/2 teaspoon almond extract
- 1   package (10 ounces) frozen puff pastry shells, thawed
- 2   small ripe pears, peeled and thinly sliced
- 1/2 teaspoon ground cinnamon
- 1/8 teaspoon ground ginger
- 1/2 cup slivered almonds, toasted, optional

In a small saucepan, combine the egg, 1/2 cup sugar, cream and butter. Cook and stir until sauce is thickened and a thermometer reads 160°. Remove from the heat; stir in extract. Cover and refrigerate.

On an unfloured surface, roll each pastry into a 4-in. circle. Place in an ungreased 15-in. x 10-in. x 1-in. baking pan. Top each with pear slices. Combine the cinnamon, ginger and remaining sugar; sprinkle over the pears.

Bake at 400° for 20 minutes or until pastry is golden brown. Sprinkle with almonds if desired. Serve warm with chilled cream sauce. **yield: 6 servings.**

raspberry chocolate puffs

raspberry chocolate puffs

Anneliese Deising • Plymouth, Michigan
This is my "show-off" dessert because it makes a spectacular presentation. Every time I serve it, my friends rave about this fun and fancy treat. Although it looks like you fussed, the recipe is actually quite simple.

  1 **cup vanilla *or* white chips**
  1 **cup milk chocolate chips**
  1 **cup chopped pecans**
  1 **package (17.3 ounces) frozen puff pastry, thawed**
  1 **package (12 ounces) frozen unsweetened raspberries, thawed**
  1 **cup confectioners' sugar**
Fresh raspberries, raspberry chips, additional vanilla chips and confectioners' sugar, optional

In a large bowl, combine chips and pecans; set aside. On a lightly floured surface, roll each pastry sheet into a 12-in. square. Cut in half lengthwise and widthwise, making eight 6-in. squares. Spoon the chip mixture in the center of each square. Pull all corners together below the tips of the corners, forming a pouch. Fold the corner tips down. Place on an ungreased baking sheet. Bake at 425° for 18-20 minutes or until golden brown. Remove to a wire rack to cool.

In a food processor, puree raspberries and confectioners' sugar. Strain and discard seeds. Spoon raspberry sauce onto dessert plates; top with pastry pouches. If desired, garnish with the raspberries and chips; dust with confectioners' sugar. **yield: 8 servings.**

sugared raisin pear diamonds

Jeanne Allen • Rye, Colorado
With their tender golden crust and tempting pear and raisin filling, these fabulous bars stand out on any buffet table. Substitute apples for the pears, and you'll still get mouth-watering results!

2-1/2 **cups plus 4-1/2 teaspoons all-purpose flour, *divided***
  1/4 **cup plus 6 tablespoons sugar, *divided***
  1/2 **teaspoon salt**
  3/4 **cup cold butter, cubed**
  1/2 **teaspoon grated lemon peel**
  1/2 **cup half-and-half cream**
    6 **cups diced peeled ripe pears (about 7)**
    6 **tablespoons golden raisins**
  1/4 **cup lemon juice**
  1/8 **to 1/4 teaspoon ground cinnamon**
    1 **egg, lightly beaten**
Additional sugar

In a large bowl, combine 2-1/2 cups flour, 1/4 cup sugar and salt. Cut in butter and lemon peel until the mixture resembles coarse crumbs. Gradually add cream, tossing with a fork until dough forms a ball.

Divide in half. On a large piece of lightly floured waxed paper, roll out one portion of dough into a 16-in. x 11-1/2-in. rectangle. Transfer to an ungreased 15-in. x 10-in. x 1-in. baking pan.

Bake at 350° for 10-15 minutes or until lightly browned. Cool on a wire rack. Increase temperature to 400°.

sugared raisin pear diamonds

In a large bowl, combine the pears, raisins, lemon juice, cinnamon and remaining flour and sugar. Spread over crust. Roll out remaining dough into a 16-in. x 12-in. rectangle; place over filling. Trim and seal edges. Brush top with egg; sprinkle with additional sugar.

Bake for 30-34 minutes or until golden brown. Cool on a wire rack. Cut into diamond-shaped bars. **yield: about 2 dozen.**

berry whirligig

Pearl Stanford • Medford, Oregon

Golden whirligigs float on a fresh blackberry sauce in this delectable dessert. I love making this for guests during the hot summer months for a cool and refreshing treat. Mix it up by serving it with a variety of your favorite berries.

sugary dessert shells

1/2	cup sugar
2	tablespoons cornstarch
1/2	teaspoon salt
1/4	teaspoon ground cinnamon
1	cup water
3	cups fresh *or* frozen blackberries *or* a mixture of berries

WHIRLIGIGS:

1	cup all-purpose flour
2	teaspoons baking powder
1/2	teaspoon salt
2	tablespoons shortening
1	egg, lightly beaten
2	tablespoons milk
1/4	cup butter, softened
1/2	cup sugar
1	teaspoon grated lemon peel
1/4	teaspoon ground cinnamon

In a large saucepan, combine the sugar, cornstarch, salt and cinnamon. Stir in water until smooth. Cook until mixture boils and thickens. Stir in berries; cook over low heat for 5 minutes.

Pour into a greased 8-in. square baking pan; set aside. In a large bowl, combine the flour, baking powder and salt. Cut in shortening until coarse crumbs form.

In a small bowl, mix egg and milk. Add to flour mixture; stir until mixture forms a soft ball. Knead several minutes. Roll into a 12-in. x 8-in. rectangle. Spread with butter. Combine sugar, peel and cinnamon; sprinkle over dough.

Starting at a long end, roll up; seal edges. Cut into 9 slices. Place slices over berry mixture. Bake at 400° for 22-25 minutes or until golden brown. **yield: 9 servings.**

sugary dessert shells

Taste of Home Test Kitchen • Greendale, Wisconsin

These light and flaky shells look impressive but are quick and easy to prepare. Centered with a creamy filling of your choice and topped with fruit, they make a great dessert or snack.

2	egg whites
1/2	cup sugar
1/4	cup butter, melted
1/2	teaspoon vanilla extract
1/2	cup all-purpose flour

Pudding, mousse *or* ice cream

Fresh fruit

Line a baking sheet with parchment paper. Draw two 6-in. circles on paper; set aside. In a small bowl, beat egg whites on medium speed until soft peaks form. Gradually beat in sugar, 1 tablespoon at a time, on high until stiff peaks form. Beat in the butter and vanilla. Gradually beat in flour until smooth.

Spoon 2 tablespoons of batter over each parchment paper circle; spread with the back of a spoon to cover circle. Bake at 350° for 8-9 minutes or until edges are lightly browned.

Remove from the paper with a metal spatula and immediately place each over an inverted 6-oz. custard cup or small bowl; shape around cup. Repeat with remaining batter to make six more shells (parchment paper can be reused). Fill with pudding and fruit. **yield: 8 servings.**

strudel sticks

Louise Holmes • Winchester, Tennessee
I like to prepare these pretty fruit- and coconut-filled pastries in advance and freeze them until needed.

- 1 cup cold butter, cubed
- 2 cups all-purpose flour
- 1/2 cup sour cream
- 1 egg, *separated*
- 1 cup peach *or* apricot preserves, *divided*
- 30 vanilla wafers, crushed
- 1/2 cup flaked coconut
- 20 pecan halves

GLAZE:
- 1/2 cup confectioners' sugar
- 1/8 teaspoon vanilla extract
- 2 to 3 teaspoons milk

In a large bowl, cut butter into flour until the mixture resembles coarse crumbs. Combine sour cream and egg yolk; add to flour mixture, stirring with a fork to form a soft dough. Divide in half; wrap in plastic wrap. Refrigerate several hours or overnight.

On a floured surface, roll each portion of dough into a 12-in. square. Spread with preserves. Combine crushed wafers and coconut; sprinkle over preserves.

Roll up jelly-roll style; seal seam. Place seam side down on a greased baking sheet. Cut widthwise with a sharp knife three-fourths of the way through dough every 1 in. Beat egg white until foamy; brush over pastry. Place a pecan half on each slice.

Bake at 350° for 25-30 minutes or until golden brown. Combine the confectioners' sugar, vanilla and enough milk to achieve desired consistency; drizzle over pastries. **yield: 2 pastries (10 servings each).**

strudel sticks

fruit crepes

fruit crepes

Jean Murtagh • Solon, Ohio
Everyone at the table will feel special eating these sweet and fruity sensations. My rich and delicate crepes are as fast to make as they are fabulous.

- 2 egg whites
- 2/3 cup fat-free milk
- 2 teaspoons canola oil
- 1/2 cup all-purpose flour
- 1/4 teaspoon salt
- 1/4 cup reduced-sugar orange marmalade
- 1 cup unsweetened raspberries, blackberries *or* blueberries

Sugar substitute equivalent to 8 teaspoons sugar
- 1/2 cup fat-free sour cream
- 1/8 teaspoon ground cinnamon

In a large bowl, combine the egg whites, milk and oil. Combine flour and salt; add to milk mixture and mix well. Cover and refrigerate for 1 hour. In a large saucepan, heat marmalade until melted; remove from the heat. Fold in berries and sugar substitute; set aside. In a small bowl, combine sour cream and cinnamon; set aside.

Heat an 8-in. nonstick skillet coated with cooking spray; add 2 tablespoons batter. Lift and tilt pan to evenly coat bottom. Cook until top appears dry and bottom is light brown. Remove to a wire rack. Repeat with remaining batter.

Spread each crepe with 1 tablespoon sour cream mixture; roll up and place in an ungreased 11-in. x 7-in. baking dish. Spoon the fruit mixture over top. Bake, uncovered, at 375° for 15 minutes. **yield: 4 servings.**

almond puff pastries

Barbara Harrison • Monte Sereno, California
My husband comes from a family of almond growers, so I often use almonds in my baking. These puff pastries have a crisp topping and creamy filling.

- 1 package (17.3 ounces) frozen puff pastry, thawed
- 1 egg, *separated*
- 1 tablespoon water
- 1 cup sliced almonds
- 1 cup sugar
- 2 cups heavy whipping cream, whipped
- Confectioners' sugar

Unfold pastry sheets onto a lightly floured surface. Cut each sheet into nine 3-in. squares. Place 1 in. apart on greased baking sheets; set aside. In a small bowl, beat egg yolk and water; brush over pastry squares. In another bowl, beat egg white; add almonds and sugar. Spread over each square.

Bake at 375° for 20-25 minutes or until well puffed and browned. Cool completely on wire racks.

Split pastries in half horizontally. Fill with whipped cream; replace tops. Sprinkle with confectioners' sugar. Serve immediately. **yield: 18 servings.**

apple cinnamon turnovers

Robin Stevens • Cadiz, Kentucky
Refrigerated biscuit dough speeds up the prep work of these wonderful turnovers. Sprinkled with cinnamon and sugar, they get rave reviews at potlucks.

- 1 medium tart apple, peeled and chopped
- 1/2 cup applesauce
- 3/4 teaspoon ground cinnamon, *divided*
- Dash ground nutmeg
- 1 tube (7-1/2 ounces) refrigerated biscuits
- 1 tablespoon butter, melted
- 2 tablespoons sugar

In a large bowl, combine the apple, applesauce, 1/4 teaspoon cinnamon and nutmeg. Separate biscuits; roll out each into a 6-in. circle.

Place on a greased baking sheet. Place a heaping tablespoonful of apple mixture in the center of each. Fold in half and pinch edges to seal. Brush with butter.

Combine the sugar and remaining cinnamon; sprinkle over tops.

Bake at 400° for 8-10 minutes or until edges are golden brown. Serve warm. **yield: 10 servings.**

pumpkin doughnut drops

Beva Staum • Muscoda, Wisconsin
I always have a few special treats handy when my grandchildren visit. These cake doughnuts are a favorite snack.

- 2 eggs
- 1-1/4 cups sugar
- 2 tablespoons shortening
- 1 cup canned pumpkin
- 2 teaspoons white vinegar
- 1 teaspoon vanilla extract
- 3 cups all-purpose flour
- 1/2 cup nonfat dry milk powder
- 3 teaspoons baking powder
- 1/2 teaspoon salt
- 1/2 teaspoon ground cinnamon
- 1/2 teaspoon ground nutmeg
- 1/2 cup lemon-lime soda
- Oil for deep-fat frying
- Additional sugar

In a large bowl, beat the eggs, sugar and shortening. Add the pumpkin, vinegar and vanilla. Combine the dry ingredients; add to the pumpkin mixture alternately with soda.

In an electric skillet or deep-fat fryer, heat oil to 375°. Drop teaspoonfuls of batter, a few at a time, into hot oil. Fry for 1 minute on each side or until golden brown. Drain on paper towels; roll in sugar while warm. **yield: about 7 dozen.**

pumpkin doughnut drops

bite-sized bliss

lemon tea cakes, p. 85

Taste of Home Desserts

Add sweet magic to all of your dessert platters with these irresistibly munchable petite treats. This chapter offers a bonanza of cookies, bars, cupcakes, tartlets, tea cakes and other lip-smacking small wonders bursting with scrumptious flavor. Whip up any of these yummy delights to nibble on whenever a craving calls or to enjoy leisurely over a cup of hot tea or cocoa.

chocolate cupcakes

chocolate cupcakes

Marlene Martin
Country Harbour Mines, Nova Scotia

If you like chocolate, you're going to fall in love with these blissful cupcakes. Chocolate curls are a showy way to garnish these gorgeous gems.

1/2	cup butter, softened
1	cup sugar
1	egg
1	teaspoon vanilla extract
1-1/2	cups all-purpose flour
1/2	cup baking cocoa
1	teaspoon baking soda
1/4	teaspoon salt
1/2	cup water
1/2	cup buttermilk

Frosting of your choice

In a small bowl, cream butter and sugar until light and fluffy. Beat in egg and vanilla. Combine the flour, cocoa, baking soda and salt; gradually add to creamed mixture alternately with water and buttermilk, beating well after each addition.

Fill paper-lined muffin cups two-thirds full. Bake at 375° for 12-15 minutes or until a toothpick inserted near the center comes out clean. Cool for 10 minutes before removing from pans to wire racks to cool completely. Frost cupcakes. **yield: 16 cupcakes.**

apricot white fudge

Debbie Purdue • Westland, Michigan

This fudge has become a family favorite because of the luscious blending of flavors. I like to make it for gifts at Christmastime.

1-1/2	teaspoons plus 1/2 cup butter, *divided*
2	cups sugar
3/4	cup sour cream
12	squares (1 ounce *each*) white baking chocolate, chopped
1	jar (7 ounces) marshmallow creme
3/4	cup chopped dried apricots
3/4	cup chopped walnuts

Line a 9-in. square pan with foil and grease with 1-1/2 teaspoons butter; set aside. In a heavy saucepan, combine sugar, sour cream and remaining butter. Bring to a boil over medium heat, stirring constantly. Cook and stir until a candy thermometer reads 234° (soft-ball stage), about 5-1/2 minutes.

Remove from the heat. Stir in chocolate until melted. Stir in marshmallow creme until blended. Fold in apricots and walnuts. Pour into prepared pan. Cover and refrigerate overnight. Using foil, lift fudge out of pan. Discard foil; cut fudge into 1-in. squares. **yield: about 2 pounds.**

editor's note: We recommend that you test your candy thermometer before each use by bringing water to a boil; the thermometer should read 212°. Adjust your recipe temperature up or down based on your test.

apricot white fudge

fancy peanut butter cookies

fancy peanut butter cookies

DESSERT *Tip*

Some recipes call for a pinch of this or a dash of that. So just what is the difference? Traditionally, a pinch is thought to be the amount of a dry ingredient that can be held between your thumb and forefinger. A dash is a very small amount of seasoning that is added with a quick downward stroke of the hand. In both cases, it is somewhere between 1/16 and a scant 1/8 teaspoon.

*Janet Hooper
Emporium,
Pennsylvania*
I always receive compliments on these moist and chewy peanut butter cookies. I frost them to add an extra-special touch.

fancy peanut butter cookies

    1   cup shortening
    1   cup peanut butter
    1   cup sugar
    1   cup packed brown sugar
    2   eggs
  1/4   cup milk
    2   teaspoons vanilla extract
3-1/2   cups all-purpose flour
    2   teaspoons baking soda
    1   teaspoon salt
FROSTING:
  1/4   cup butter, softened
  1/4   cup shortening
  1/4   cup peanut butter
    4   cups confectioners' sugar
  1/4   cup milk
    1   teaspoon vanilla extract

Dash salt
ICING:
  1/2   cup semisweet chocolate chips, melted
    2   tablespoons milk

In a large bowl, cream the shortening, peanut butter and sugars until light and fluffy. Add eggs, one at a time, beating well after each addition. Beat in milk and vanilla. Combine the flour, baking soda and salt; gradually add to the creamed mixture and mix well.

Roll into 1-in. balls. Place 2 in. apart on ungreased baking sheets. Bake at 375° for 10-12 minutes or until golden brown. Remove to wire racks.

For frosting, in a large bowl, cream the butter, shortening, peanut butter and confectioners' sugar until light and fluffy. Beat in the milk, vanilla and salt until smooth. Frost cookies. Combine melted chips and milk; drizzle over frosting. **yield: 7-1/2 dozen.**

editor's note: Reduced-fat or generic brands of peanut butter are not recommended for this recipe.

cranberry crisps

Sandy Furches • Lake City, Florida
I developed this recipe after sampling a similar cookie while traveling in North Carolina. These pretty cookies keep well in the freezer, so I always have some on hand for midday munching.

1	cup butter-flavored shortening
1	cup sugar
1	cup packed brown sugar
2	eggs
2	teaspoons vanilla extract
2-1/2	cups old-fashioned oats
2	cups all-purpose flour
1	teaspoon baking soda
1	teaspoon ground cinnamon
1/2	teaspoon salt
1/2	teaspoon baking powder
1-1/3	cups dried cranberries
1	cup coarsely chopped walnuts

In a large bowl, cream shortening and sugars until light and fluffy. Add eggs, one at a time, beating well after each addition. Beat in vanilla. Combine the oats, flour, baking soda, cinnamon, salt and baking powder; gradually add to the creamed mixture and mix well. Stir in the cranberries and walnuts.

Drop by tablespoonfuls 2 in. apart onto lightly greased baking sheets. Bake at 350° for 12-14 minutes or until lightly browned. Remove to wire racks to cool. **yield: 5 dozen.**

cranberry crisps

frosted peanut butter bars

frosted peanut butter bars

Sharon Smith • Muskegon, Michigan
These sweet, chewy bars are a great no-fuss treat to bring to a potluck or bake sale. A drizzle of chocolate on top makes for a pretty presentation.

1/3	cup shortening
1/2	cup peanut butter
1-1/2	cups packed brown sugar
2	eggs
1	teaspoon vanilla extract
1-1/2	cups all-purpose flour
1-1/2	teaspoons baking powder
1/2	teaspoon salt
1/4	cup milk

FROSTING:

2/3	cup creamy peanut butter
1/2	cup shortening
4	cups confectioners' sugar
1/3	to 1/2 cup milk

TOPPING:

1/4	cup semisweet chocolate chips
1	teaspoon shortening

In a large bowl, cream the shortening, peanut butter and brown sugar until light and fluffy. Beat in eggs and vanilla. Combine the flour, baking powder and salt; gradually add to creamed mixture alternately with milk, beating well after each addition.

Transfer to a greased 15-in. x 10-in. x 1-in. baking pan. Bake at 350° for 16-20 minutes or until a toothpick inserted near the center comes out clean. Cool on a wire rack.

For frosting, in a small bowl, cream the peanut butter, shortening and confectioners' sugar until light and fluffy. Gradually beat in enough milk to achieve spreading consistency. Frost bars.

In a microwave, melt chocolate chips and shortening; stir until smooth. Drizzle over frosting. Store in the refrigerator. **yield: 5 dozen.**

chocolate raspberry bars

Diana Olmstead • Yelm, Washington
A boxed cake mix and raspberry jam simplify assembly of these sweet treats. The bars are very rich, so cut them into small pieces.

- 1   package (18-1/4 ounces) devil's food cake mix
- 1   egg
- 1/3 cup butter, softened
- 1   jar (12 ounces) seedless raspberry jam
- **TOPPING:**
- 1   package (10 to 12 ounces) vanilla *or* white chips
- 1   package (8 ounces) cream cheese, softened
- 2   tablespoons milk
- 1/2 cup semisweet chocolate chips
- 2   tablespoons butter

In a large bowl, combine the dry cake mix, egg and butter until crumbly. Press into a greased 15-in. x 10-in. x 1-in. baking pan.

Bake at 350° for 8-10 minutes or until a toothpick inserted near the center comes out clean (crust will appear puffy and dry). Cool on a wire rack. Spread jam over the crust.

In a microwave, melt vanilla chips at 70% power for 1 minute; stir. Microwave at additional 10- to 20-second intervals, stirring until smooth. In a large bowl, beat cream cheese and milk until smooth. Stir in melted chips. Carefully spread over jam.

In a microwave, melt chocolate chips and butter; stir until smooth. Drizzle or pipe over the cream cheese layer. Refrigerate before cutting. **yield: about 6 dozen.**

lemon tea cakes

Charlene Crump • Montgomery, Alabama
Whenever I serve these lovely bite-size glazed cakes, they get rave reviews…and I get requests for the recipe. Lemon and cream cheese make for a winning combination.

- 1-1/2 cups butter, softened
- 1   package (8 ounces) cream cheese, softened
- 2-1/4 cups sugar
- 6   eggs
- 3   tablespoons lemon juice
- 2   teaspoons lemon extract
- 1   teaspoon vanilla extract
- 1-1/2 teaspoons grated lemon peel
- 3   cups all-purpose flour
- **GLAZE:**
- 5-1/4 cups confectioners' sugar
- 1/2 cup plus 3 tablespoons milk
- 3-1/2 teaspoons lemon extract

In a large bowl, cream the butter, cream cheese and sugar until light and fluffy. Add eggs, one at a time, beating well after each addition. Beat in the lemon juice, extracts and lemon peel. Add flour; beat just until moistened.

Fill greased miniature muffin cups two-thirds full. Bake at 325° for 10-15 minutes or until a toothpick comes out clean. Cool for 5 minutes before removing from pans to wire racks to cool completely.

In a small bowl, combine glaze ingredients. Dip tops of cakes into glaze; place on waxed paper to dry. **yield: 8-1/2 dozen.**

lemon tea cakes

caramel swirls

Jan Smith • Star, Texas

In my opinion, cookies are the best dessert to make and to eat! With a crisp outside and chewy caramel filling, these cookies are some of my favorites.

1	cup butter, softened
4	ounces cream cheese, softened
1	cup packed brown sugar
1	egg yolk
1	teaspoon maple flavoring
2-3/4	cups all-purpose flour

FILLING:

30	caramels
2	packages (3 ounces *each*) cream cheese, softened

In a large bowl, cream the butter, cream cheese and brown sugar until light and fluffy. Beat in egg yolk and maple flavoring. Gradually add flour and mix well. Refrigerate for 2 hours or until easy to handle.

In a microwave-safe bowl, melt caramels; stir until smooth. Stir in cream cheese until blended; set aside. Divide dough in half. Roll each portion between waxed paper to 1/4-in. thickness. Spread caramel mixture over dough to within 1/2 in. of edges.

Roll up tightly jelly-roll style, starting with a long side. Wrap rolls in plastic wrap; refrigerate for 4 hours or until firm.

Unwrap and cut into 1/4-in. slices. Place 1 in. apart on greased baking sheets. Bake at 350° for 12-14 minutes or until golden brown. Remove to wire racks to cool. **yield: 6-1/2 dozen.**

coconut peaks

Patricia Shinn • Fruitland Park, Florida

I found this gem on a slip of paper in a cookbook I got at a yard sale. The candies get great flavor from browned butter.

1/4	cup butter
3	cups flaked coconut
2	cups confectioners' sugar
1/4	cup half-and-half cream
1	cup (6 ounces) semisweet chocolate chips
2	teaspoons shortening

Line a baking sheet with waxed paper; set aside. In a large saucepan, cook butter over medium-low heat until golden brown, about 5 minutes. Remove from the heat; stir in the coconut, sugar and cream.

Drop by rounded teaspoonfuls onto prepared baking sheet. Refrigerate until easy to handle, about 25 minutes.

Roll mixture into balls, then shape each into a cone. Return to baking sheet; refrigerate for 15 minutes.

Meanwhile, in a microwave, melt chocolate chips and shortening; stir until smooth. Dip bottoms of cones into chocolate; allow excess to drip off. Return to waxed paper to harden. Store in an airtight container in the refrigerator. **yield: about 3 dozen.**

maple cream bonbons

Ginny Truwe • Mankato, Minnesota

My family always smiles when I fix these chocolates. They recall the winter when I put trays of the candy centers on top of my van in the garage to freeze before dipping. Later, I drove off and was horrified to see the little balls rolling on the highway!

1	cup butter, softened
3-1/2	cups confectioners' sugar
3	tablespoons maple flavoring
2	cups chopped walnuts
2	cups semisweet chocolate chips
1	cup butterscotch chips

In a large bowl, cream the butter, sugar and maple flavoring until smooth. Stir in walnuts. Shape into 1-in. balls; place on waxed paper-lined baking sheets. Freeze until firm.

In a microwave, melt the chips; stir until smooth. Dip balls in chocolate; allow excess to drip off. Place on waxed paper-lined baking sheets. Refrigerate until set. Store in the refrigerator. **yield: 5 dozen.**

apple nut bars

apple nut bars

Karen Nelson • Sullivan, Wisconsin
Try these goodies if you're looking for big apple taste packed into a yummy bar. An added bonus…you don't have to peel any apples.

- 2 egg whites
- 2/3 cup sugar
- 1/2 teaspoon vanilla extract
- 1/2 cup all-purpose flour
- 1 teaspoon baking powder
- 2 cups chopped tart apples
- 1/4 cup chopped pecans

In a large bowl, whisk the egg whites, sugar and vanilla for 1-1/2 minutes or until frothy. Whisk in flour and baking powder until blended. Fold in apples and chopped pecans.

Transfer to a 9-in. square baking pan coated with cooking spray. Bake at 350° for 22-28 minutes or until a toothpick inserted near the center comes out clean. Cool on a wire rack. **yield: 1 dozen.**

easy cherry tarts

Frances Poste • Wall, South Dakota
Refrigerated crescent rolls simplify the preparation of these delightful cherry bites. To keep things easy, cut the dough into circles with a small juice glass.

- 1 tube (8 ounces) refrigerated crescent rolls
- 1 package (3 ounces) cream cheese, softened
- 1/4 cup confectioners' sugar
- 1 cup canned cherry pie filling
- 1/4 teaspoon almond extract

Place crescent dough on a lightly floured surface; seal seams and perforations. Cut into 2-in. circles. Place in greased miniature muffin cups. In a small bowl, beat cream cheese and confectioners' sugar until smooth. Place about 1/2 teaspoon in each cup. Combine pie filling and extract; place about 2 teaspoons in each cup.

Bake at 375° for 12-14 minutes or until edges are lightly browned. Remove to wire racks to cool. Refrigerate until serving. **yield: 2 dozen.**

candied cherry nut bars

Barbara Wilson • Thamesville, Ontario
The mixture of nuts, cherries and chocolate chips makes these sweet treats a colorful addition to any dessert platter.

- 1-1/4 cups all-purpose flour
- 2/3 cup packed brown sugar, *divided*
- 3/4 cup cold butter, cubed
- 1 egg
- 1/2 teaspoon salt
- 1-1/2 cups salted mixed nuts
- 1-1/2 cups halved green and red candied cherries
- 1 cup (6 ounces) semisweet chocolate chips

In a small bowl, combine flour and 1/3 cup brown sugar; cut in butter until mixture resembles coarse crumbs. Press into a lightly greased 13-in. x 9-in. baking pan. Bake at 350° for 15-17 minutes or until set.

In a large bowl, beat the egg, salt and remaining brown sugar until blended. Stir in the nuts, cherries and chocolate chips. Spoon evenly over crust.

Bake 20-25 minutes longer or until topping is set. Cool on a wire rack before cutting. **yield: 3 dozen.**

candied cherry nut bars

DESSERT *Tip*

You can whip up a batch of cupcakes in no time with one of these three quick and easy ways to fill cupcake liners or muffin tins. One simple way is to pour the batter into a large resealable plastic bag, snip off a corner and squeeze the batter into the liners or tins. Another great idea is to use a dry measuring cup if the batter is thin or a spring-loaded ice cream scoop if the batter is thick. Any of these filling methods will assure that the cupcake batter is divided evenly, and even better yet, there will be no mess to clean up afterwards!

Paula Zsiray
Logan, Utah
These crowd-pleasing cupcakes are quick, moist and yummy. Take just one bite and you'll see why they disappear fast!

chocolate chip cupcakes

- 1 **package (18-1/4 ounces) yellow cake mix**
- 1 **package (3.4 ounces) instant vanilla pudding mix**
- 1 **cup water**
- 1/2 **cup canola oil**
- 4 **eggs**
- 1 **cup (6 ounces) miniature semisweet chocolate chips**
- 1 **can (16 ounces) chocolate *or* vanilla frosting**

Additional miniature semisweet chocolate chips, optional

In a large bowl, combine the cake and pudding mixes, water, oil and eggs; beat on low speed for 30 seconds. Beat on medium for 2 minutes. Stir in chocolate chips.

Fill paper-lined muffin cups two-thirds full. Bake at 375° for 18-22 minutes or until a toothpick inserted near the center comes out clean. Cool for 10 minutes before removing to wire racks to cool completely. Frost cupcakes. Sprinkle with additional chocolate chips if desired. **yield: 2-1/2 dozen.**

orange cappuccino creams

Lucile Cline • Wichita, Kansas
As holiday gifts, these mocha-orange morsels are sure to be a sweet success. The delighted response they get is well worth the kitchen time it takes to make them.

12	squares (1 ounce *each*) white baking chocolate, chopped
6	tablespoons heavy whipping cream, *divided*
1-1/2	teaspoons orange juice
1/2	teaspoon orange extract
1-1/2	teaspoons finely grated orange peel
1/4	cup finely chopped walnuts
2	teaspoons instant coffee granules
4	squares (1 ounces *each*) semisweet chocolate, chopped

In a small heavy saucepan over low heat, melt white chocolate with 1/4 cup cream, orange juice, extract and peel. Stir until chocolate is melted. Remove from the heat; stir in walnuts. Cool for 10-12 minutes.

Using a small spoon, fill paper or foil candy cups about two-thirds full with cooled chocolate mixture. Chill for 30 minutes.

Meanwhile, in a small saucepan, combine coffee granules and remaining cream. Cook and stir over low heat until coffee is dissolved. Add semisweet chocolate; cook and stir until chocolate is melted. Spoon about 1/2 teaspoon over each cup. Store in an airtight container at room temperature. **yield: about 4 dozen.**

orange cappuccino creams

hint o' mint cookies

hint o' mint cookies

Janet Hartmann • Gibbon, Minnesota
With a little peppermint extract, these tender, cake-like cookies bring a nice close to any meal.

1/2	cup butter, softened
1	cup sugar
1	egg
1/2	teaspoon vanilla extract
1/4	teaspoon peppermint extract
2	cups all-purpose flour
1/2	teaspoon baking soda
1/4	teaspoon cream of tartar
1/2	cup buttermilk

FROSTING:

3	tablespoons butter, softened
2	cups confectioners' sugar
1/3	cup baking cocoa
1/8	teaspoon salt
1	teaspoon vanilla extract
2	to 4 tablespoons milk

In a large bowl, cream butter and sugar until light and fluffy. Beat in egg and extracts. Combine the flour, baking soda and cream of tartar; add to the creamed mixture alternately with buttermilk, beating well after each addition. Cover and refrigerate for 1 hour or until easy to handle.

Drop by heaping teaspoonfuls 2 in. apart onto ungreased baking sheets. Flatten with a glass dipped in sugar. Bake at 350° for 6 to 8 minutes or until set. Remove to wire racks to cool.

In a small bowl, beat the butter, sugar, cocoa, salt, vanilla and enough milk to achieve spreading consistency. Frost cookies. **yield: 4 dozen.**

frosted pumpkin cookies

frosted pumpkin cookies

Leona Luttrell • Sarasota, Florida
These family favorites taste so good, it's hard to eat just one! They freeze and travel well, especially if you let the icing completely dry, then layer the cookies between sheets of waxed paper.

- 1 cup shortening
- 2 cups packed brown sugar
- 1 can (15 ounces) solid-pack pumpkin
- 4 cups all-purpose flour
- 2 teaspoons baking powder
- 2 teaspoons baking soda
- 2 teaspoons ground cinnamon
- 1/8 teaspoon salt
- 1 cup chopped pecans
- 1 cup chopped dates

CARAMEL FROSTING:
- 1/2 cup butter, cubed
- 1-1/2 cups packed brown sugar
- 1/4 cup milk
- 1 teaspoon maple flavoring
- 1/2 teaspoon vanilla extract
- 2 to 2-1/2 cups confectioners' sugar

In a large bowl, cream shortening and brown sugar until light and fluffy. Beat in pumpkin. Combine the flour, baking powder, baking soda, cinnamon and salt; gradually add to pumpkin mixture and mix well. Stir in pecans and dates.

Drop by rounded teaspoonfuls 2 in. apart onto ungreased baking sheets. Bake at 375° for 13-15 minutes or until firm.

Meanwhile, for frosting, combine the butter, brown sugar and milk in a small saucepan. Bring to a boil over medium heat, stirring constantly; boil for 3 minutes. Remove from the heat; stir in the maple flavoring and vanilla.

Cool slightly; beat in enough confectioners' sugar to achieve spreading consistency. Remove cookies to wire racks; frost while warm. **yield: 6-1/2 dozen.**

caramel creams

Barbara Yongers • Kingman, Kansas
These cookies are delicious plain, but I like to make them into sandwich cookies with the brown butter filling. In a pinch, use a can of store-bought frosting instead of making your own from scratch.

- 1 cup butter, softened
- 2/3 cup packed brown sugar
- 2 egg yolks
- 1/2 teaspoon vanilla extract
- 2-1/2 cups all-purpose flour
- 1/3 cup finely chopped pecans
- 1/4 teaspoon salt

FILLING:
- 2 tablespoons plus 1-1/2 teaspoons butter
- 1-1/2 cups confectioners' sugar
- 1/2 teaspoon vanilla extract
- 2 to 3 tablespoons heavy whipping cream

In a large bowl, cream butter and brown sugar until light and fluffy. Beat in egg yolks and vanilla. Combine

caramel creams

the flour, pecans and salt; gradually add to the creamed mixture and beat well. Shape into two 10-in. rolls; wrap each in plastic wrap. Refrigerate for 1-2 hours.

Unwrap and cut into 1/4-in. slices. Place 2 in. apart on ungreased baking sheets. Bake at 350° for 11-13 minutes or until golden brown. Remove to wire racks to cool.

For filling, in a small saucepan, cook butter over medium heat until golden brown. Pour into a large bowl, beat in the confectioners' sugar, vanilla and enough cream to achieve spreading consistency. Spread on the bottom of half of the cookies; top with remaining cookies. **yield: about 3 dozen.**

chocolate marshmallow meltaways

Joanna Swartley • Harrisonburg, Virginia
Kids are thrilled to find a marshmallow hidden under this cookie's cocoa frosting. I enjoyed these cookies as a child, and now my own family loves them, too.

1/2	cup butter-flavored shortening
3/4	cup sugar
1	egg
1/4	cup milk
1	teaspoon vanilla extract
1-3/4	cups all-purpose flour
1/2	cup baking cocoa
1/2	teaspoon salt
1/2	teaspoon baking soda
18	large marshmallows, halved

FROSTING:

3	tablespoons butter, softened
3	cups confectioners' sugar
3	tablespoons baking cocoa
1/8	teaspoon salt
4	to 6 tablespoons milk

In a large bowl, cream shortening and sugar until light and fluffy. Beat in the egg, milk and vanilla. Combine the flour, cocoa, salt and baking soda; gradually add to creamed mixture and mix well.

Drop by tablespoonfuls 2 in. apart onto ungreased baking sheets. Bake at 350° for 8 minutes. Press a marshmallow half, cut side down, onto each cookie; bake 2 minutes longer. Remove to wire racks to cool.

In a small bowl, beat the butter, confectioners' sugar, cocoa and salt until smooth. Add enough milk to achieve a spreading consistency. Frost cookies. **yield: 3 dozen.**

terrific toffee

terrific toffee

Carol Gillespie • Chambersburg, Pennsylvania
This buttery toffee is one of those must-make treats my family requests for the holidays. You can also try variations to make English or Hazelnut Toffee.

1-1/2	teaspoons plus 1 cup butter, *divided*
1	cup semisweet chocolate chips
1	cup milk chocolate chips
1	cup sugar
3	tablespoons water
2	cups coarsely chopped almonds, toasted, *divided*

Butter a large baking sheet with 1-1/2 teaspoons butter; set aside. In a small bowl, combine semisweet and milk chocolate chips; set aside.

In a heavy saucepan, combine the sugar, water and remaining butter. Cook and stir over medium heat until a candy thermometer reaches 290° (soft-crack stage). Remove from the heat; stir in 1 cup almonds. Immediately pour onto prepared baking sheet.

Sprinkle with chocolate chips; spread with a knife when melted. Sprinkle with remaining almonds. Let stand until set, about 1 hour. Break into 2-in. pieces. Store in an airtight container. **yield: about 2 pounds.**

editor's note: We recommend that you test your candy thermometer before each use by bringing water to a boil; the thermometer should read 212°. Adjust your recipe temperature up or down based on your test.

peanut butter fingers

Margie Lowry • McCammon, Idaho

Always a hit with the teenagers in our house, these rich bars are sure to please the peanut butter lovers in your family. They're great for serving at holiday time.

- 3/4 cup butter, softened
- 3/4 cup creamy peanut butter
- 3/4 cup sugar
- 3/4 cup packed brown sugar
- 2 eggs
- 1-1/2 teaspoons vanilla extract
- 1-1/2 cups all-purpose flour
- 1-1/2 cups quick-cooking oats
- 3/4 teaspoon baking soda
- 1/2 teaspoon salt
- 1 cup (6 ounces) semisweet chocolate chips

GLAZE:
- 3/4 cup creamy peanut butter
- 1 cup confectioners' sugar
- 4 to 6 tablespoons milk
- 1 cup chopped peanuts

In a large bowl, cream the butter, peanut butter and sugars until light and fluffy. Add eggs, one at a time, beating well after each addition. Beat in vanilla. Combine the flour, oats, baking soda and salt; add to creamed mixture and mix well. Pour into a greased 15-in. x 10-in. x 1-in. baking pan.

peanut butter fingers

Bake at 325° for 18-20 minutes or until a toothpick inserted near the center comes out clean. Immediately sprinkle with chocolate chips. Allow chips to soften for a few minutes, then spread over bars.

For glaze, in a small bowl, beat peanut butter and confectioners' sugar until smooth. Add enough milk to achieve spreading consistency. Carefully spread over warm bars; sprinkle with peanuts. Cool before cutting into bars. **yield: 5 dozen.**

editor's note: Reduced-fat or generic brands of peanut butter are not recommended for this recipe.

apple pie tartlets

Mary Kelley • Minneapolis, Minnesota

Sweet and cinnamony, these mouth-watering morsels are a delightful addition to a dessert buffet or snack tray. For extra convenience, you can even prebake the shells a day or two in advance.

- 1 sheet refrigerated pie pastry
- 1 tablespoon sugar

Dash ground cinnamon

FILLING:
- 2 teaspoons butter
- 2 cups diced peeled tart apples
- 3 tablespoons sugar
- 3 tablespoons fat-free caramel ice cream topping
- 2 tablespoons all-purpose flour
- 1/2 teaspoon ground cinnamon
- 1/2 teaspoon lemon juice
- 1/8 teaspoon salt

Roll out pastry on a lightly floured surface; cut into twenty 2-1/2-in. circles. Press onto the bottom and up the sides of miniature muffin cups coated with cooking spray. Prick pastry with a fork. Spray lightly with cooking spray. Combine the sugar and cinnamon; lightly sprinkle over pastry.

Bake at 350° for 6-8 minutes or until golden brown. Cool for 5 minutes before removing from pans to wire racks.

In a large saucepan, melt butter. Add the apples; cook and stir over medium heat for 4-5 minutes or until crisp-tender.

Stir in the sugar, caramel topping, flour, cinnamon, lemon juice and salt. Bring to a boil; cook and stir for 2 minutes or until sauce is thickened and apples are tender. Cool for 5 minutes. Spoon into tart shells. **yield: 10 servings.**

white chocolate peanut butter squares

Gloria Jarrett • Tall Pines Farm, Loveland, Ohio

People regularly request the recipe once they try this peanut butter fudge dipped in melted white chocolate. It's a nice contrast to typical chocolates on a candy platter.

1	tablespoon plus 3/4 cup butter, *divided*
3	cups sugar
2/3	cup evaporated milk
1	package (10 ounces) peanut butter chips
1	jar (7 ounces) marshmallow creme
1	cup chopped nuts
1	tablespoon vanilla extract
1-1/2	pounds white candy coating
1/2	cup semisweet chocolate chips, optional
1	teaspoon shortening, optional

Line a 13-in. x 9-in. pan with foil. Grease the foil with 1 tablespoon butter; set aside. In a heavy saucepan, combine the sugar, evaporated milk and remaining butter. Bring to a boil over medium heat; cook and stir for 5 minutes. Remove from the heat; stir in the peanut butter chips until melted. Add the marshmallow creme, nuts and vanilla; stir until blended. Pour into prepared pan. Cool.

Remove from pan and cut into 1-in. squares. Place on waxed paper-lined baking sheets; freeze or refrigerate until firm.

In a microwave, melt candy coating; stir until smooth. Dip the squares into the coating; place on waxed paper-lined baking sheets until set.

white chocolate peanut butter squares

old-fashioned caramels

In a microwave, melt chocolate chips and shortening if desired; stir until smooth. Drizzle over the squares. Store in an airtight container. **yield: 3-1/4 pounds (about 9-1/2 dozen).**

old-fashioned caramels

Jan Batman • Oskaloosa, Iowa

Before I was married, my future father-in-law would fix these creamy caramels at Christmas and send me some. The recipe has been in my husband's family for decades...so, when we got married, I learned to make them, too.

1	tablespoon plus 1 cup butter, *divided*
2	cups sugar
1-3/4	cups light corn syrup
2	cups half-and-half cream
1	teaspoon vanilla extract
1	cup chopped pecans, optional

Line an 11-in. x 7-in. pan with foil; grease with 1 tablespoon butter and set aside.

In a large heavy saucepan over medium heat, combine the sugar, corn syrup and remaining butter. Bring to a boil, stirring constantly; boil gently for 4 minutes without stirring. Remove from the heat; stir in cream. Reduce heat to medium-low and cook until a candy thermometer reads 238° (soft-ball stage), stirring constantly. Remove from the heat; stir in vanilla and pecans if desired.

Pour into prepared pan; cool. Remove from pan and cut into 1-in. squares. **yield: about 6 dozen.**

editor's note: We recommend that you test your candy thermometer before each use by bringing water to a boil; the thermometer should read 212°. Adjust your recipe temperature up or down based on your test.

melts in your mouth

raspberry-fudge frozen dessert, p. 101

Taste of Home Desserts

If your palate is pleased with anything featuring a texture that's soft, smooth or creamy, then you're sure to fall in love with the original dessert creations in the pages that follow. Get the inside scoop on how to whip up these tantalizing recipes for pudding, mousse, ice cream, fondue, parfaits and other luscious indulgences that are guaranteed to dazzle family and friends.

frozen ice cream delight

frozen ice cream delight

Susan Bracken • Apex, North Carolina

This recipe is a refreshing summer treat that dates back to before "fast food" ice cream. It's also handy—you can make it days ahead of time.

2-1/2 cups cream-filled chocolate sandwich cookie crumbs, *divided*
1/2 cup butter, melted
1/2 cup sugar
1/2 gallon chocolate, coffee *or* vanilla ice cream, softened
2 cups confectioners' sugar
2/3 cup semisweet chocolate chips
1/2 cup butter, cubed
1 can (12 ounces) evaporated milk
1 teaspoon vanilla extract
1-1/2 cups salted peanuts
1 carton (8 ounces) frozen whipped topping, thawed

Combine 2 cups cookie crumbs with butter and sugar. Press onto the bottom of a 13-in. x 9-in. dish. Freeze for 15 minutes.

Spread ice cream over crumbs; freeze until firm, about 3 hours.

In a small saucepan, combine the confectioners' sugar, chocolate chips, butter and evaporated milk. Bring to a boil; boil for 8 minutes. Remove from the heat; stir in vanilla. Cool to room temperature.

Spoon chocolate sauce over the ice cream layer; sprinkle with peanuts. Freeze until firm. Spread whipped topping over the top; sprinkle with remaining cookie crumbs. Freeze for at least 3 hours before serving. **yield: 12-16 servings.**

dessert from the grill

Becky Gillespie • Boulder, Colorado

I complete grilled meals with this light, refreshing dessert. By the time we're done eating, the coals have cooled to the right temperature. I brush slices of pineapple and pound cake with a yummy sauce, toast them on the grill and top them with ice cream and convenient caramel sauce.

1 can (20 ounces) sliced pineapple rings, drained
1 teaspoon butter
1/2 teaspoon brown sugar
1/4 teaspoon vanilla extract
1/8 teaspoon ground cinnamon
1/8 teaspoon ground nutmeg
6 slices pound cake
Vanilla ice cream
Caramel ice cream topping

Drain pineapple, reserving 1/3 cup juice and six pineapple rings (save remaining juice and pineapple for another use).

In a microwave-safe dish, combine the butter, brown sugar, vanilla, cinnamon, nutmeg and reserved pineapple juice. Microwave, uncovered, on high for 1-2 minutes or until bubbly. Brush half of the mixture on both sides of pineapple rings and cake slices.

Grill, uncovered, over medium heat. Cook pineapple and cake for 1-2 minutes on each side or until golden brown, brushing occasionally with remaining pineapple juice mixture.

Top each slice of cake with a pineapple ring and scoop of ice cream; drizzle with caramel topping. Serve immediately. **yield: 6 servings.**

dessert from the grill

banana split brownie pie

Tanna Walker
Salina, Kansas
I often use Neapolitan in place of three different ice cream flavors to make this luscious dessert. You can bake the brownie crust days ahead, top it with the ice cream and freeze until you're ready to serve.

banana split brownie pie

4 ounces German sweet chocolate, chopped
1/2 cup butter, cubed
3 eggs
1 cup sugar
1/2 teaspoon vanilla extract
1/2 cup all-purpose flour
1-1/3 cups vanilla ice cream
1-2/3 cups chocolate ice cream
1-2/3 cups strawberry ice cream
2 medium firm bananas, sliced
1 cup fresh strawberries, sliced
1/2 to 3/4 cup hot fudge ice cream topping, warmed
1/2 to 3/4 cup strawberry ice cream topping
1/4 to 1/2 cup toffee bits *or* almond brickle chips
Whipped cream and sliced almonds

In a microwave, melt chocolate and butter; stir until smooth. Cool. In a small bowl, beat the eggs, sugar, vanilla and chocolate mixture. Gradually add flour until well blended. Spread into a greased 9-in. springform pan.

Bake brownie crust at 350° for 30-35 minutes or until a toothpick inserted near the center comes out clean. Cool on a wire rack. Cover and freeze until firm.

Using 1/3 cup for each scoop, place four scoops of vanilla ice cream, five scoops of chocolate ice cream and five scoops of strawberry ice cream on a waxed paper-lined baking sheet. Freeze until firm. Place vanilla scoops in center of brownie crust; alternate scoops of chocolate and strawberry around edge. Cover and freeze until firm.

Just before serving, remove sides of pan. Arrange the bananas and strawberries over ice cream. Drizzle with hot fudge and strawberry toppings. Sprinkle with toffee bits. Garnish with whipped cream and almonds. Cut into wedges. **yield: 10 servings.**

fancy phyllo cups

Cody Geisler • Minnetonka, Minnesota

Phyllo dough is great for making eye-catching desserts such as these whimsical cups. Experiment with other preserves for a tasty twist on these fancy sweet treats.

8   sheets phyllo dough (14 inches x 9 inches)
1/3 cup butter, melted
1/2 cup confectioners' sugar
1/2 cup vanilla *or* white chips
2   tablespoons milk
1   package (8 ounces) cream cheese, softened
1   carton (8 ounces) frozen whipped topping, thawed
1/2 cup seedless raspberry preserves, room temperature
White chocolate curls, optional

Place one sheet of phyllo dough on a work surface (keep remaining phyllo covered with plastic wrap and a damp towel to prevent it from drying out); brush sheet with butter and dust with confectioners' sugar. Top with a second sheet of phyllo; brush with butter and dust with sugar.

Cut into 12 squares. Place one square on top of a second square, alternating corner points; press into a greased muffin cup. Repeat with remaining 10 squares, filling five more muffin cups. Repeat the process three times with remaining phyllo dough, butter and sugar.

Bake at 350° for 5-6 minutes or until lightly browned. Carefully remove from pans to wire racks to cool.

fancy phyllo cups

In a microwave, melt the vanilla chips and milk at 70% power for 1 minute; stir. Microwave at additional 10- to 20-second intervals, stirring until smooth. In a large bowl, beat cream cheese and melted chip mixture until smooth. Fold in whipped topping.

Spoon or pipe into phyllo cups; drizzle with raspberry preserves. Cover and refrigerate until serving. Garnish with chocolate curls if desired. **yield: 2 dozen.**

old-fashioned rice pudding

Laura German • North Brookfield, Massachusetts

I was fortunate to grow up around fabulous cooks. My mother and grandmother taught me to experiment with recipes, and we tried a lot of variations on this one. No matter how we chose to embellish it, it was always tasty.

1   cup cooked long grain rice
1   cup milk
5   teaspoons sugar
Dash salt
1/2 teaspoon vanilla extract
Whipped cream, optional

In a small saucepan, combine the rice, milk, sugar and salt. Cook, uncovered, over medium heat for 20 minutes or until thickened, stirring often. Remove from the heat; stir in vanilla. Spoon into serving dishes. Serve warm; top with whipped cream if desired. **yield: 2 servings.**

peanutty chocolate pudding

Naomi Giddis • Two Buttes, Colorado

I jazz up instant chocolate pudding by stirring in a small amount of peanut butter. The smooth results are sure to satisfy the dessert lovers in your family.

2   cups cold fat-free milk
1   package (1.4 ounces) sugar-free instant chocolate (fudge) pudding mix
1/3 cup reduced-fat peanut butter
Fat-free whipped topping

In a large bowl, beat the milk and pudding mix for 2 minutes. Let stand for 2 minutes or until soft set. Beat in peanut butter until smooth. Spoon into dessert dishes. Top with whipped topping if desired. **yield: 4 servings.**

white chocolate bread pudding

Kathy Rundle • Fond du Lac, Wisconsin
A delectable white chocolate sauce is the crowning touch on servings of this comforting cinnamon bread pudding.

16	slices cinnamon bread, crusts removed, cubed
1	cup dried cranberries
3/4	cup vanilla *or* white chips
3/4	cup chopped pecans
1/4	cup butter, melted
6	eggs
4	cups milk
3/4	cup plus 1 tablespoon sugar, *divided*
1	teaspoon vanilla extract
1/4	teaspoon ground cinnamon
1/4	teaspoon ground allspice

SAUCE:

2/3	cup heavy whipping cream
2	tablespoons butter
8	squares (1 ounce *each*) white baking chocolate, chopped

In a greased 13-in. x 9-in. baking dish, layer half of the bread cubes, cranberries, vanilla chips and pecans. Repeat layers. Drizzle with butter.

In a large bowl, beat the eggs, milk, 3/4 cup sugar, vanilla, cinnamon and allspice until blended; pour over bread mixture. Let stand for 15-30 minutes.

Sprinkle with remaining sugar. Bake, uncovered, at 375° for 55-65 minutes or until a knife inserted near the

white chocolate bread pudding

freezer peanut butter pie

center comes out clean. Cover loosely with foil during the last 15 minutes if top browns too quickly.

In a small saucepan, bring cream and butter to a boil. Add chocolate and remove from the heat (do not stir). Let stand for 5 minutes; whisk until smooth. Serve sauce with warm bread pudding. **yield: 12 servings (1-1/2 cups sauce).**

freezer peanut butter pie

Nina Rufener • Mansfield, Ohio
This pie can be assembled in a jiffy and pulled out of the freezer the next time you need a quick dessert. A ribbon of peanut butter in the center makes it oh-so scrumptious.

1	quart vanilla ice cream, softened
1	graham cracker crust (9 inches)
1/2	cup peanut butter
1/3	cup light corn syrup

Chocolate syrup
Chopped walnuts

Spread half of the ice cream into crust. Combine peanut butter and corn syrup; spread over ice cream. Top with remaining ice cream. Drizzle with chocolate syrup and sprinkle with nuts.

Cover and freeze for 3-4 hours. Remove from the freezer 15 minutes before serving. **yield: 6-8 servings.**

lacy fruit cups with sabayon sauce

lacy fruit cups with sabayon sauce

Taste of Home Test Kitchen • Greendale, Wisconsin
This fruity dessert from our home economists is a refreshing change of pace from other heavy desserts.

- 3 tablespoons butter
- 3 tablespoons brown sugar
- 3 tablespoons light corn syrup
- 2 tablespoons plus 2 teaspoons all-purpose flour
- 1/3 cup ground pecans
- 1/4 teaspoon vanilla extract
- 5 egg yolks
- 1/2 cup rose *or* marsala wine
- 1/3 cup sugar
- 2 medium pink grapefruit, peeled and sectioned
- 2 medium blood oranges *or* tangerines, peeled and sectioned
- 3/4 cup fresh raspberries

In a small saucepan, melt butter over low heat. Stir in brown sugar and corn syrup; cook and stir until mixture comes to a boil. Remove from the heat. Stir in flour. Fold in pecans and vanilla.

Drop by tablespoonfuls 3 in. apart onto parchment paper-lined baking sheets. Bake at 325° for 8-10 minutes or until golden brown. Cool for 30-60 seconds. Working quickly, peel the cookies off paper and immediately drape over inverted 6-oz. custard cups; cool completely.

In a small saucepan, combine the egg yolks, wine and sugar. Cook and stir over medium heat until mixture

reaches 160° or is thick enough to coat the back of a metal spoon.

Divide the grapefruit, oranges and berries among cookie cups; top with sauce. Serve immediately. **yield: 8 servings.**

editor's note: If the cookies become firm before they are draped over custard cups, warm them on the baking sheet for 1 minute to soften.

peanut butter chocolate fondue

Beverly Olthaus • Cincinnati, Ohio
This warm fondue is great to serve with fruit or cake cubes for dessert or while we're watching football games on Sunday afternoons. It really warms us up.

- 1 cup (6 ounces) semisweet chocolate chips
- 1/2 cup sugar
- 1/2 cup milk
- 1/2 cup creamy peanut butter
- 4 large firm bananas, cut into 3/4-inch slices
- 1 pint whole strawberries

In a heavy saucepan, cook and stir the chocolate chips, sugar, milk and peanut butter over low heat until smooth. Transfer to a fondue pot and keep warm. Serve with bananas and strawberries. **yield: 12 servings.**

berry cheesecake parfaits

Joyce Mart • Wichita, Kansas
I can serve up this easy dessert in no time. Impressive and delicious, it seems to be just the right touch after a full meal. I also recommend it as a great midnight snack.

- 1 package (8 ounces) cream cheese, softened
- 2 to 4 tablespoons sugar
- 1/2 cup vanilla yogurt
- 2 cups fresh raspberries *or* berries of your choice
- 1/2 cup graham cracker crumbs (8 squares)

In a large bowl, beat cream cheese and sugar until smooth. Stir in yogurt.

In four dessert glasses or bowls, alternate layers of berries, cream cheese mixture and cracker crumbs. Serve immediately or refrigerate for up to 8 hours. **yield: 4 servings.**

raspberry-fudge frozen dessert

raspberry-fudge frozen dessert

Sue Kroening • Mattoon, Illinois
This frozen specialty always receives a big "thumbs-up" from all who taste it. The combination of vanilla, raspberry and chocolate fudge flavors will melt in your mouth.

- 2 **cups vanilla ice cream, partially softened**
- 1/2 **cup chopped pecans, toasted**
- 2 **cups raspberry sherbet *or* sorbet, partially softened**
- 2 **cups chocolate fudge ice cream, partially softened**
- 1 **package (10 ounces) frozen sweetened raspberries, thawed**
- 2 **cups (12 ounces) semisweet chocolate chips**
- 1/4 **cup butter, cubed**
- 1/2 **cup light corn syrup**
- 1/2 **cup water**

Fresh raspberries, optional

Line the bottom and sides of a 9-in. x 5-in. loaf pan with plastic wrap. Combine vanilla ice cream and pecans; spread into prepared pan. Freeze for 30 minutes.

Spread raspberry sherbet over ice cream. Freeze for 30 minutes. Spread chocolate ice cream over the top. Cover and freeze for 8 hours or until firm.

Mash and strain raspberries, reserving 1/4 cup juice (discard seeds and save remaining raspberry juice for another use). In a microwave-safe bowl, melt chocolate chips and butter; stir until smooth. Whisk in the corn syrup, water and reserved raspberry juice; cool.

Remove dessert from the freezer 10 minutes before serving. Using plastic wrap, remove loaf from pan; discard plastic wrap. Using a serrated knife, cut ice cream into 12 slices. Spoon chocolate sauce onto dessert plates; top with ice cream. Garnish with fresh raspberries if desired. **yield: 12 servings.**

strawberry banana dessert

Margaret Kuntz • Bismarck, North Dakota
Like springtime on a plate, this eye-catching dessert has a bright cheery color and plenty of fruity flavor.

- 3 **medium firm bananas, sliced**
- 1 **prepared angel food cake (16 ounces), cut into 1-inch cubes**
- 1 **pint fresh strawberries, halved**
- 1 **package (.6 ounce) sugar-free strawberry gelatin**
- 2 **cups boiling water**
- 1-1/2 **cups cold water**
- 1 **carton (8 ounces) reduced-fat whipped topping, thawed**

Layer banana slices and cake cubes in a 13-in. x 9-in. dish coated with cooking spray. Place strawberries over cake and press down gently.

In a small bowl, dissolve gelatin in boiling water; stir in cold water. Pour over strawberries. Refrigerate for 3 hours or until set. Frost with whipped topping. **yield: 16 servings.**

strawberry banana dessert

DESSERT *Tip*

Popular in England, lemon curd is a soft custard that's often used as a tart filling. The custard is made from lemon juice, sugar, eggs and butter. The flavor and texture, however, are similar to lemon meringue pie filling. The simple ingredients are cooked together until they become thickened. After the mixture has cooled, it can be used as a filling for baked desserts or as a spread for scones, biscuits or other baked goods.

Taste of Home
Test Kitchen
Greendale, Wisconsin
Homemade tart lemon curd balances the light meringue cups and rich chocolate ganache in these desserts.

chocolaty lemon meringue cups

chocolaty lemon meringue cups

MERINGUE:
- 2 **egg whites**
- 1/2 **teaspoon vanilla extract**
- 1/4 **teaspoon salt**
- 1/4 **teaspoon white vinegar**
- 1/2 **cup sugar**
- 1/4 **cup miniature semisweet chocolate chips**

LEMON CURD:
- 6 **eggs**
- 2 **cups sugar**
- 1 **cup lemon juice (about 4 lemons)**
- 1/2 **cup butter, melted**
- 2 **tablespoons grated lemon peel**

GANACHE:
- 4 **squares (1 ounce** *each***) semisweet chocolate, coarsely chopped**
- 1/2 **cup heavy whipping cream**
- 1/2 **teaspoon vanilla extract**

For meringue, in a large bowl, beat the egg whites, vanilla, salt and vinegar on medium speed until soft peaks form. Gradually beat in sugar, 1 tablespoon at a time, on high until stiff peaks form. Fold in chocolate chips.

Drop meringue into eight mounds on parchment paper-lined baking sheets. Shape into 3-in. cups with the back of a spoon.

Bake at 275° for 45 minutes or until set and dry. Turn oven off; leave meringues in oven for 1-1/2 hours.

Meanwhile, in a large heavy saucepan, combine eggs and sugar. Stir in the lemon juice, butter and lemon peel. Cook and stir over medium-low heat for 15 minutes or until mixture is thickened and reaches 160°. Transfer to a small bowl; refrigerate until chilled.

For ganache, in a small saucepan, melt the chocolate with cream over low heat; stir until blended. Remove from the heat; stir in the vanilla. Cool slightly.

Just before serving, spoon lemon curd into meringue cups. Drizzle ganache around meringue. **yield: 8 servings.**

tiramisu parfaits

Nancy Granaman • Burlington, Iowa

As a mouth-watering finale, I whip up this tiramisu and serve it in pretty parfait glasses. I think they look so pretty with a drizzle of chocolate or cocoa on top.

- 4-1/2 teaspoons instant coffee granules
- 1/3 cup boiling water
- 2 cups cold fat-free milk
- 2 packages (1 ounce *each*) sugar-free instant vanilla pudding mix
- 4 ounces fat-free cream cheese
- 1 package (3 ounces) ladyfingers, split and cubed
- 2 cups fat-free whipped topping
- 2 tablespoons miniature chocolate chips
- 1 teaspoon baking cocoa

Dissolve coffee in boiling water; cool to room temperature. In a large bowl, whisk milk and pudding mixes for 2 minutes. Let stand for 2 minutes or until soft-set. In another large bowl, beat cream cheese until smooth. Gradually fold in pudding.

Place ladyfinger cubes in a bowl. Add coffee; toss to coat. Let stand for 5 minutes.

Divide half of the ladyfinger cubes among six parfait glasses or serving dishes. Top with half of the pudding mixture, 1 cup whipped topping and 1 tablespoon chocolate chips. Repeat layers.

Cover and refrigerate for 8 hours or overnight. Just before serving, dust with cocoa. **yield: 6 servings.**

meringue berry pie

tiramisu parfaits

meringue berry pie

Page Alexander • Baldwin City, Kansas

A hot day calls for a cool dessert like this tempting pie. Fresh berries and a sweet raspberry sauce over ice cream in a meringue crust make each slice absolutely irresistible.

MERINGUE:
- 1/2 cup sugar, *divided*
- 1/4 cup slivered almonds, toasted and ground
- 2 tablespoons cornstarch
- 2 egg whites
- 1/8 teaspoon cream of tartar

SAUCE AND TOPPING:
- 1/2 cup sugar
- 1 tablespoon cornstarch
- 1/3 cup water
- 1 pint fresh raspberries
- 1 quart vanilla ice cream
- 2 cups mixed fresh berries

For meringue, in a small bowl, combine 1/4 cup sugar, almonds and cornstarch; set aside. In a large bowl, beat egg whites and cream of tartar on medium speed until soft peaks form. Gradually beat in remaining sugar, 1 tablespoon at a time, on high until stiff peaks form. Fold in almond mixture. Spread evenly over the bottom and up the sides of a greased 9-in. pie plate.

Bake at 275° for 1 to 1-1/2 hours or until light golden brown. Turn oven off; leave meringues in oven for 1 hour. Cool on a wire rack.

For sauce, combine sugar and cornstarch in a large saucepan. Gradually stir in water until smooth; add raspberries. Bring to a boil over medium heat; cook and stir for 1 minute or until thickened. Set aside to cool.

Scoop ice cream into crust; top with mixed berries and sauce. Freeze leftovers. **yield: 6-8 servings.**

strawberry meringue desserts

from the paper and store in an airtight container at room temperature.

In a microwave, melt chocolate chips and shortening; stir until smooth. Spread 1 tablespoon over each meringue. Let stand until chocolate is set.

In a large bowl, beat cream until soft peaks form. Gradually add confectioners' sugar and remaining vanilla, beating on high until stiff peaks form.

Set aside 12 strawberries; cut remaining strawberries into 1/4-in. slices. Place 12 meringues on a flat serving platter. Spread each with 2 tablespoons whipped cream; top with sliced strawberries. Spread each with 2 tablespoons whipped cream. Top with remaining meringues and whipped cream. Loosely cover; refrigerate for up to 2 hours.

Just before serving, drizzle desserts with chocolate syrup. Cut reserved strawberries in half. Arrange cut side down over whipped cream. Refrigerate leftovers. **yield: 12 servings.**

strawberry meringue desserts

Susan Maraffa • Canfield, Ohio
This fluffy treat is one you won't be able to pass up. When time is short, use thawed whipped topping instead of making sweetened whipped cream.

4	egg whites
1-1/2	teaspoons vanilla extract, *divided*
1/4	teaspoon cream of tartar
1/8	teaspoon salt
1	cup sugar
1	cup (6 ounces) semisweet chocolate chips
4	teaspoons shortening
2	cups heavy whipping cream
2	tablespoons confectioners' sugar
5	cups fresh strawberries

Chocolate syrup

Line baking sheets with parchment paper. Draw twenty-four 4-in. x 2-1/2-in. rectangles on the paper; set aside.

For meringue, in a large bowl, beat the egg whites, 1 teaspoon vanilla, cream of tartar and salt on medium speed until soft peaks form. Gradually beat in sugar, 1 tablespoon at a time, on high until stiff peaks form.

Insert a #12 round pastry tip in a pastry bag or heavy-duty plastic bag. Fill bag with meringue. Pipe meringue in long rows on rectangles until each is completely filled. Bake at 250° for 1 hour or until set and dry. Turn oven off; leave meringues in oven for 1 hour.

Remove from the oven and cool on baking sheets. When cooled completely, remove the meringues

hot chocolate souffles

Taste of Home Test Kitchen • Greendale, Wisconsin
These individual chocolate souffles from our home economists are fudgy and delicious. They look impressive but are actually quite easy to make.

1	cup butter, cubed
8	squares (1 ounce *each*) bittersweet chocolate, chopped

hot chocolate souffles

4 eggs
4 egg yolks
1-1/2 cups plus 2 tablespoons sugar
2 tablespoons all-purpose flour
1/8 teaspoon baking powder
1 cup miniature marshmallows
4-1/2 teaspoons cinnamon-sugar

Grease the bottoms only of twelve 6-oz. ramekins or custard cups; set aside. In a large microwave-safe bowl, melt butter and chocolate; stir until smooth. Set aside.

In a large bowl, beat the eggs and yolks on high speed for 3 minutes or until light and fluffy. Gradually add the sugar, beating until thick and lemon-colored, about 5 minutes. Beat in the chocolate mixture. Combine the flour and baking powder; beat into egg mixture just until combined.

Fill prepared ramekins half full; sprinkle with miniature marshmallows. Bake at 400° for 12-15 minutes or until a toothpick inserted near the center comes out with moist crumbs. Sprinkle with cinnamon-sugar; serve immediately. Refrigerate leftovers. **yield: 12 servings.**

caramel pear pudding

Sharon Mensing • Greenfield, Iowa
Don't expect this old-fashioned dessert to last long. The delicate pears and irresistible caramel topping make it a winner whenever I serve it.

1 cup all-purpose flour
2/3 cup sugar
1-1/2 teaspoons baking powder
1/2 teaspoon ground cinnamon
1/4 teaspoon salt
Pinch ground cloves
1/2 cup milk
4 medium pears, peeled and cut into 1/2-inch cubes
1/2 cup chopped pecans
3/4 cup packed brown sugar
1/4 cup butter
3/4 cup boiling water
Vanilla ice cream *or* whipped cream, optional

In a large bowl, combine the first six ingredients; beat in milk until smooth. Stir in pears and pecans. Spoon into an ungreased 2-qt. baking dish.

In another bowl, combine the brown sugar, butter and water; pour over batter. Bake, uncovered, at 375° for 45-50 minutes. Serve warm with ice cream or whipped cream if desired. **yield: 8 servings.**

white chocolate parfaits

white chocolate parfaits

Jennifer Eilts • Lincoln, Nebraska
This very elegant dessert is great served on a warm summer night or at a dinner party. You can substitute other types of berries until you find your favorite combination.

3/4 cup heavy whipping cream
1/4 cup sugar
2 teaspoons cornstarch
2 egg yolks
4 squares (1 ounce *each*) white baking chocolate
1 teaspoon vanilla extract
3 cups whipped topping
1-1/2 cups fresh blueberries
1-1/2 cups fresh raspberries
Sliced strawberries and additional whipped topping, optional

In a large saucepan, combine the cream, sugar and cornstarch. Cook and stir over medium heat until mixture reaches 160° or is thick enough to coat the back of a metal spoon.

Stir a small amount into egg yolks; return all to the pan, stirring constantly. Bring to a gentle boil; cook and stir for 2 minutes; stir in chocolate until melted. Remove from the heat; gently stir in vanilla.

Cool mixture to room temperature, about 15 minutes. Fold in whipped topping. Place 1/4 cup each in four parfait glasses.

Combine blueberries and raspberries; place 1/4 cup in each glass. Repeat layers of chocolate mixture and berries twice. Cover and refrigerate for at least 1 hour. Garnish with strawberries and whipped topping if desired. **yield: 4 servings.**

old-fashioned ice cream roll

Darlene Brenden • Salem, Oregon
Frozen swirls of cake and ice cream drizzled with a luscious caramel sauce and sprinkled with pecans make this a dazzling dessert. It's worth the extra effort to be able to share this time-honored treat.

    4   eggs
    3/4 cup sugar
    1   teaspoon vanilla extract
    3/4 cup all-purpose flour
    3/4 teaspoon baking powder
    1/4 teaspoon salt
    1/2 gallon vanilla ice cream, slightly softened
CARAMEL SAUCE:
    1   cup packed brown sugar
    1/2 cup sugar
    1/4 teaspoon salt
    1/2 cup light corn syrup
    1   cup heavy whipping cream
Chopped pecans, optional

Line a greased 15-in. x 10-in. x 1-in. baking pan with waxed paper. Grease the paper; set aside. In a large bowl, beat eggs for 3 minutes. Gradually add sugar; beat for 2 minutes or until mixture becomes thick and lemon-colored. Beat in vanilla. Combine dry ingredients; fold into egg mixture.

Spread batter evenly into prepared pan. Bake at 375° for 10-12 minutes or until cake springs back when lightly touched. Cool for 5 minutes. Invert onto a kitchen towel dusted with confectioners' sugar. Gently peel off waxed paper. Roll up cake in the towel jelly-roll

old-fashioned ice cream roll

chocolate cream dessert

style, starting with a short side. Cool completely on a wire rack.

Spread cooled cake with ice cream; roll up again. Freeze until firm.

For sauce, in a small saucepan, combine the sugars, salt and corn syrup. Cook and stir until mixture comes to a boil. Remove from the heat; cool slightly. Stir in cream. Serve with ice cream roll. Sprinkle with pecans if desired. **yield: 8-10 servings (2 cups sauce).**

Variation: Use strawberry ice cream instead of vanilla and eliminate caramel sauce. Garnish with fresh strawberries and whipped cream.

chocolate cream dessert

Pam Reddell • Linden, Wisconsin
This dessert makes a cool and delicious treat on a warm summer day. Simply bake a tender crust from a cake mix, then layer it with a cream cheese blend, chocolate pudding and whipped topping.

    3/4 cup cold butter, cubed
    1   package (18-1/4 ounces) chocolate cake mix
    1   egg, lightly beaten
    1   package (8 ounces) cream cheese, softened
    1   cup confectioners' sugar
    4   cups whipped topping, *divided*
    3   cups cold milk
    2   packages (3.9 ounces *each*) instant chocolate
        pudding mix
    2   tablespoons chocolate curls

In a bowl, cut butter into cake mix until crumbly. Add egg and mix well. Press into a greased 13-in. x 9-in. baking dish. Bake at 350° for 15-18 minutes or until set. Cool completely on a wire rack.

In a small bowl, beat cream cheese and confectioners' sugar until smooth. Fold in 1 cup of whipped topping. Carefully spread over the crust; refrigerate.

In a large bowl, whisk the milk and pudding mix for 2 minutes; let stand for 2 minutes or until soft-set. Spread over the cream cheese layer. Top with the remaining whipped topping. Refrigerate for 2 hours before cutting. Garnish with chocolate curls. Refrigerate leftovers. **yield: 12 servings.**

easy trifle for two

Betty Kibbe • Albuquerque, New Mexico
Since there are just the two of us in the house now, I take a "keep it small" approach to my cooking and baking. This trifle helps me do just that. The vanilla wafers work perfectly for small-portion desserts.

- 16 vanilla wafers
- 2 tablespoons raspberry preserves
- 1/2 cup prepared vanilla pudding
- 2 tablespoons flaked coconut, toasted
- 1/3 cup prepared tapioca pudding

Spread the flat side of 12 wafers with 1/2 teaspoon raspberry preserves each. Crumble remaining wafers and set aside.

Place five wafers each around the edges of two individual 4- to 6-oz. dishes, preserves side facing in. Place one wafer in the bottom of each dish, preserves side up. Spoon vanilla pudding in the center; sprinkle with wafer crumbs and half of the coconut. Top with tapioca pudding and remaining coconut. Cover and refrigerate for at least 3 hours. **yield: 2 servings.**

flan

Kathy Gilligan • Phoenix, Arizona
This light egg custard recipe comes from a missionary friend who lives in Mexico. It's very typical of the Southwest...and very delicious!

- 8 eggs, lightly beaten
- 2/3 cup sugar
- 1/4 teaspoon salt
- 2 cans (12 ounces *each*) evaporated milk
- 2 teaspoons vanilla
- 1/2 cup brown sugar

In a large bowl, combine the eggs, sugar and salt. Stir in milk and vanilla. Sift brown sugar into eight 5-oz.

custard cups or a 1-1/2-qt. baking dish. Pour custard mixture over sugar.

Place in shallow baking pan of hot water. Bake at 325° for 30-40 minutes or until knife inserted near center comes out clean. Chill overnight. Sprinkle with additional brown sugar before serving or unmold to serve. **yield: 12 servings.**

butter crunch pudding

Kathy Giesbrecht • Prespatou, British Columbia
You'll need just four ingredients to make the sweet crumb topping for this dessert. This is one of those scrumptious recipes that can be whipped up in a jiffy and still earn you oohs and aahs as if you spent all day in the kitchen.

- 1 cup all-purpose flour
- 1/2 cup flaked coconut
- 1/4 cup packed brown sugar
- 1/2 cup cold butter
- 2 cups cold milk
- 1 package (3.4 ounces) instant lemon pudding mix *or* flavor of your choice

In a large bowl, combine flour, coconut and brown sugar; cut in butter until crumbly. Spread the crumb mixture on a 15-in. x 10-in. x 1-in. baking pan. Bake at 375° for 15 minutes, stirring once. Cool slightly.

Meanwhile, in another large bowl, whisk milk and pudding mix for 2 minutes. Let stand for 2 minutes or until soft-set; chill for 5 minutes.

Spoon half of the crumbs into each of four dessert bowls. Top with pudding and remaining crumb mixture. **yield: 4 servings.**

butter crunch pudding

General Index

DOUGHNUTS & CREAM PUFFS
(also see Crepes; Pastries)
Apple Cinnamon Turnovers, 79
Blue-Ribbon Doughnuts, 73
County Fair Funnel Cakes, 70
Cream Puff Dessert, 70
Long Johns, 72
Mocha Cream Puffs, 71
Pumpkin Doughnut Drops, 79

FRUIT *(also see specific kinds)*
Fruit Crepes, 78
Lacy Fruit Cups with Sabayon
    Sauce, 100
Midsummer Sponge Cake, 65
Persimmon Nut Roll, 57
Sugary Dessert Shells, 77

ICE CREAM & SHERBET
Banana Split Brownie Pie, 97
Chocolate Ice Cream, 49
Citrus Sherbet Torte, 36
Dessert from the Grill, 96
Freezer Peanut Butter Pie, 99
Frozen Ice Cream Delight, 96
Meringue Berry Pie, 103
Mud Pie, 42
Old-Fashioned Ice Cream Roll, 106
Raspberry-Fudge Frozen Dessert, 101
Sugary Dessert Shells, 77

LEMONS & LIMES
Cherry-Lemon Icebox Pie, 16
Chocolaty Lemon Meringue Cups, 102
Citrus Sherbet Torte, 36
Classic Lemon Meringue Pie, 12
Genoise with Fruit & Cream Filling, 25
Lemon Mascarpone Cheesecake, 9
Lemon Poppy Seed Cake, 54
Lemon Tart, 15
Lemon Tea Cakes, 85
Lemonade Layer Cake, 64

MARSHMALLOWS &
MARSHMALLOW CREME
Apricot White Fudge, 82
Candy Bar Fudge, 50
Chocolate Clusters, 42
Chocolate Marshmallow Meltaways, 91
Hot Chocolate Souffles, 104
Mamie Eisenhower's Fudge, 49
Triple Chocolate Delight, 42
White Chocolate Peanut Butter
    Squares, 93

MERINGUE
Chocolaty Lemon Meringue Cups, 102
Classic Lemon Meringue Pie, 12
Meringue Berry Pie, 103
Rhubarb Meringue Pie, 19
Strawberry Meringue Desserts, 104

MINT
Candy Cane Cheesecake, 16
Hint o' Mint Cookies, 89

NUTS & PEANUT BUTTER
Almond Pear Tartlets, 75
Almond Puff Pastries, 79
Apple Nut Bars, 87
Apple Nut Cake with Rum Sauce, 55
Apple Strudel, 71
Apricot White Fudge, 82
Black Forest Torte, 37
Blueberry Graham Dessert, 33
Candied Cherry Nut Bars, 87
Caramel Creams, 90
Caramel Pear Pudding, 105
Cherry Banana Cream Pie, 10
Cherry Cream Trifle, 32
Chocolate-Almond Sacher Torte, 46
Chocolate Clusters, 42
Chocolate Cream Bonbons, 40
Chocolate Hazelnut Torte, 48
Cranberry Coffee Cake, 75
Cranberry Crisps, 84
Fancy Peanut Butter Cookies, 83
Flourless Apricot Pecan Tart, 21
Freezer Peanut Butter Pie, 99
Frosted Peanut Butter Bars, 84
Frozen Ice Cream Delight, 96
Hazelnut Pear Tart, 8
Italian Cream Cheese Cake, 54
Lacy Fruit Cups with Sabayon
    Sauce, 100
Mamie Eisenhower's Fudge, 49
Maple Cream Bonbons, 86
Meringue Berry Pie, 103
Mocha Almond Dessert, 11
Orange Cappuccino Creams, 89
Peanut Butter Apple Dessert, 26
Peanut Butter Chocolate Fondue, 100
Peanut Butter Fingers, 92
Peanutty Chocolate Pudding, 98
Pear Crunch Pie, 11
Persimmon Nut Roll, 57
Raspberry Butter Torte, 62
Raspberry-Fudge Frozen Dessert, 101
Strawberry Cheesecake Pie, 13
Sweet Potato Cake, 62
Sweetheart Trifle, 24
Terrific Toffee, 91
Triple Chocolate Delight, 42
White Chocolate Bread Pudding, 99
White Chocolate Peanut Butter
    Squares, 93

OATS & OATMEAL
Cranberry Crisps, 84
Peanut Butter Fingers, 92
Three-Layer Chocolate Brownies, 45

ORANGES & GRAPEFRUIT
Chocolate Layer Cake, 36
Citrus Sherbet Torte, 36
Fruit Crepes, 78
Lacy Fruit Cups with Sabayon
    Sauce, 100
Orange Angel Food Cake
    Dessert, 59
Orange Cappuccino Creams, 89
Orange Chocolate Torte, 26

PASTRIES *(also see Doughnuts & Cream Puffs; Meringues)*
Almond Pear Tartlets, 75
Almond Puff Pastries, 79
Apple Strudel, 71
Berry Whirligig, 77
Chocolate Eclairs, 68
Chocolate Napoleons, 73
Fancy Phyllo Cups, 98
Lacy Fruit Cups with Sabayon
    Sauce, 100
Raspberry Chocolate Puffs, 76
Strudel Sticks, 78
Sugary Dessert Shells, 77

PEACHES & PEARS
Almond Pear Tartlets, 75
Caramel Pear Pudding, 105
Hazelnut Pear Tart, 8
Pear Crunch Pie, 11
Spiced Peach Pie, 18
Strudel Sticks, 78
Sugared Raisin Pear
    Diamonds, 76

PIES *(also see Tarts)*
Banana Split Brownie Pie, 97
Blackberry Cheese Pie, 10
Cherry Banana Cream Pie, 10
Cherry-Lemon Icebox Pie, 16
Classic Lemon Meringue Pie, 12
Coconut Chiffon Pie, 18
Cran-Raspberry Pie, 17
Freezer Peanut Butter Pie, 99
Meringue Berry Pie, 103
Mud Pie, 42
Pear Crunch Pie, 11
Rhubarb Meringue Pie, 19
Spiced Peach Pie, 18
Star-Studded Blueberry Pie, 20
Strawberry Cheesecake Pie, 13
Summer Berry Pie, 19
Toffee Apple Pie, 12
Yogurt Berry Pies, 10

PINEAPPLE
Cherry Cream Trifle, 32
Dessert from the Grill, 96
Yum-Yum Cake, 35

Alphabetical Index